# Beyond The Appliqué Garden

## by Shirley Bloomfield

Enjoy!
Shirley Bloomfield
April 2016

# Dedication

With love for my daughter Claire for her inspiration and enthusiasm;
for my son Mark for his web wizardry; and for my half-Czech grandchildren,
Sammy and Sofie, to share with them part of their English heritage.

Beyond The Appliqué Garden
First published in 2013 by Teamwork Craftbooks

Text, photographs and quilt designs
© Shirley Bloomfield   Illustrations © Gail Lawther

ISBN: 978 0 9553499 7 3

British Library Cataloguing in Publication Data

A catalogue record for this book is available from
the British Library

Designed by Teamwork, Christopher and Gail Lawther
100 Wiston Avenue, Worthing, West Sussex, BN14 7PS
e-mail: thelawthers@ntlworld.com
website: www.gaillawther.co.uk

Set in Chaparral Pro, Cronos, Piranesi Italic

Printed by Foundry Press, Unit A, Foundry Lane,
Horsham, West Sussex, RH13 5PX
www.foundry-press.co.uk

# Beyond The Appliqué Garden

## Steps to success for beautiful appliqué

# by Shirley Bloomfield

TEAMWORK
CRAFTBOOKS

# Contents

# *Introduction*

*Beyond The Appliqué Garden* has been written in response to the many requests I've received for a follow-up to my first book *The Appliqué Garden*; this was published in 2006 and is now out of print. In *The Appliqué Garden* I gave detailed instructions for needle-turned appliqué, and many of the appliqué designs included were in the style of the American Baltimore Album quilts of the mid 19th century. I took this genre and gave it an English twist, inspired by the plants and wildlife in my English cottage garden.

Since then I have continued to develop this style of hand appliqué, using new techniques and creating new designs. However, I know that many quilters also like machine appliqué, so in this book you will also find tips and techniques for working the designs by machine: you can choose which method you prefer. Some designs work better by machine, others by hand, and some may be worked by either method – and you'll find that still other designs can be worked in a mix of hand and machine techniques. In the instructions for each project I've given many suggestions, so that you can choose which method(s) you prefer according to your own skill level, the ease and speed of stitching, and the final effect you want to achieve.

Both machine and hand appliqué have their own particular appeal and distinctive 'look'. Hand appliqué gives a raised, soft look, whereas machine appliqué has a crisper, flatter appearance which is also very attractive, and for some designs this would be my preferred option.
Fused, raw-edge appliqué is ideal for very small, intricate shapes; another advantage of fusing the shapes is that you can create further texture by adding different edge finishes, such as hand buttonhole stitch or machine satin stitch. Machine appliqué

(with either a turned edge or a satin stitch finish) is advisable for items such as children's quilts, which are subjected to a lot of hard wear and frequent washing.

I know that many readers of *The Appliqué Garden* found certain sections of that book especially helpful, particularly the ones covering basic needle-turned appliqué techniques and those giving advice about fabrics and equipment, so I have included a fully revised version of these sections. The section called *Appliqué Techniques* (see p14-26) includes not only the basic techniques for needle-turned appliqué but also other methods such as cut-away appliqué, faced shapes and broderie perse, as well as machine-stitched fused raw-edge appliqué. *Take a Bias Strip* (see p26-29) explains five methods for making stems, and the *Lined Appliqué* section, as you would expect, describes several ways to line your appliqué motifs. In addition, throughout the book there are many new tips and ideas to help you achieve success with appliqué.

Whichever technique you choose for your appliqué, the piece will be greatly enhanced by the way you quilt and border it. You may intend to stitch several blocks and combine them into a larger quilt, or you may choose to use a single block as a wall hanging or cushion cover.

Throughout the book I've quilted and bordered the different pieces in various ways to illustrate some of the possibilities. The section *Finishing Touches* takes you through the steps to complete your project with advice on borders, quilting and binding.

Dimensional techniques are favourites of mine, and I couldn't resist including some new ones in some of the project designs. Dimensional blooms are fun to make, and much easier to stitch than you might think from their complex appearance. The flowers have a variety of uses, and as well as incorporating them into quilts you can also use them to make great fashion accessories, and to decorate boxes or trim a bag.

As in my previous book, many of the techniques I include have been developed through teaching several hundreds of students over the years. My aim is to ensure that the techniques will work, and that students will be rewarded for all the effort, time and patience they put into their appliqué with a finished project that they are pleased with and will enjoy. I hope that you too will find the techniques in this book helpful in achieving your appliqué 'goals' – either by hand or machine or both – and that you will be encouraged to 'have a go' if you have steered away from appliqué in the past! For your first piece I would advise you not to start with anything too challenging: begin with a simple design with just a few pieces, gain confidence, and then move forward to your next project. The *Leafy Tree* project on p30 would make a good first design for practising and developing your hand- or machine-appliqué skills.

For *Beyond The Appliqué Garden* I've designed and stitched twelve new designs and projects; each one includes specific techniques to extend your skills and techniques. If you already have *The Appliqué Garden* you will find lots of new tips and techniques in this one – don't skip a section thinking you already know that part! If you don't have the earlier book, you will still find that this one works fine as a stand-alone book, with all the basics included plus much more.

Before you start a project, please take time to read through all the instructions carefully; if necessary, refer back to the first part of the book to refresh your memory on the basic techniques.

# Fabrics and Equipment

## *Fabric choices*

### Colour

There are many factors which influence our choice of fabric, but colour is probably the most important factor when we're confronted by the tremendous choice available to quilters today. The inspiration for most of my work is the natural world – plants, flowers, birds etc – so generally I try to use fabric colours that are appropriate for the subject. However, this isn't the only approach, and a couple of years ago I started to explore using taupes and a restrained colour palette (**a**), influenced by examples of beautiful Japanese appliqué and pieced quilts. There's an extensive range of these fabrics available now, in both prints and wovens; if you don't require a realistic effect, this approach can work very well for a soft, stylized look. The simple appliqué bag on p107 is an example of using this kind of colour-scheme to create a useful accessory.

**a**

### Fibre content and weave

Here your choice will be influenced by the appliqué technique you're going to use.

◇  For **needle-turned appliqué** (see p15), 100% cotton fabric – the same type used for patchwork and quilting – works best, as the fabric will crease easily to give a smooth edge to the appliqué. Look also for a fabric with a reasonably high thread count; coarser, more open-weave fabrics will fray easily, and lead to frustration! Batiks (**b**) are my favourites; not only are they closely woven (and so are very resistant to fraying), but they also come in some wonderful colours and prints which are ideal for creating shading on leaves and petals. A disadvantage is that, as the fabric *is* so closely woven, the appliqué stitch tends to sit on the surface instead of snuggling down in the weave of the fabric; however, if you use a very fine thread in a good matching colour (see p10) that will overcome this challenge.

**b**

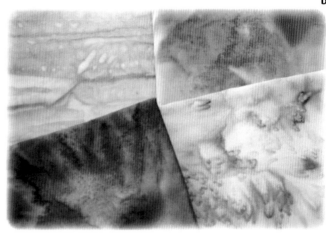

◇  If you are doing **raw-edge machined appliqué** (see p21), there's a wider choice of fabric that will work well – although it's still best to avoid fabrics which fray easily. Cotton fabrics (as described above) work well, particularly for small pieces, but you could also use rayons, silk and mixed-fibre fabrics; nets, felts and heavier cotton fabrics can also be used to create contrast textural effects. Ultra-suede™, a non-woven fabric with a suede-like appearance, is useful for very small shapes in both hand and machine appliqué.

◇  For **faced machined shapes** (see p24), such as the flowers shown (**c**), you need to use lightweight fabrics to prevent excess bulk in the seams.

◇  For **dimensional flowers** (**d**), where the flowers are generally made by gathering fabric tightly, soft lightweight cottons or lightweight silks are the best choices.

c

d

some of the lovely subtle prints in neutral shades, and I liked the effect better: it was less stark – but of course the pattern must not be too dominant, otherwise it will conflict with the appliqué design. For ideas, look at the background fabrics that I've used for the projects in this book. In recent years I've also used more coloured backgrounds. A dark background can also be used with stunning effect; light-coloured flowers really glow on a dark background (see *Midnight Dance* on p54, which is stitched on a deep blue background). There are tips later on in the book for stitching light-coloured appliqué shapes onto a dark background (see p98-99)

## To wash or not to wash!

There is always a debate about this, with different quilters having their own preferences. I personally wash all my fabrics before using them for appliqué: I have seen too many fabrics 'bleed' to risk not pre-washing. Washing will remove excess dye and sizing. I wash on a 40° synthetic programme (with no washing detergent), adding a 'dye-catcher' sheet to pick up any loose colour; I then iron the fabric while it's damp to give a crease-free finish. If I have any concerns about a fabric that still seems to bleed dye, I've found that rinsing it in a solution of Retayne™ will usually fix the problem.

# General equipment

Whether you intend to appliqué your design by hand or machine, the following list contains the most useful general pieces of equipment you will need.

## Needles

◇  For hand appliqué I prefer to use Straws or Milliners #11. These are very fine, and the extra length makes it easier to manipulate the needle. They do bend slightly in use, and when they are completely boomerang-shaped it's time to use a fresh needle!

◇  An alternative shorter needle is a Sharp #10 or 11.

◇  A needle-threader is useful for threading fine needles.

◇  For machine appliqué I use a Microtex needle; size #70 works well for the fine threads used in the projects in this book.

## Turning sticks

◇  A bamboo skewer – about 4in long – is ideal for turning under the seam allowance. You will find these skewers in grocery/kitchen departments; whittle the straight end to produce a flat shape which is useful for turning points.

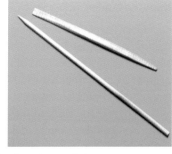

## Print and pattern

I used to hand-dye fabrics, but today there are many prints available which have a hand-dyed, random-shaded appearance. Prints which look like tie-dyed fabric have lovely colour gradations that can give realism to your appliqué designs, so if realism is what you're after look for textures, 'splashy' prints and random designs rather than regular prints. Checks, plaids, stripes and spotted fabrics, though, are fun for folk-art, highly-stylized and naïve designs. Leaf prints and bold floral designs are also useful, as you can 'fussy-cut' elements: more of that later (see p25)!

## Backgrounds

Ideally your background fabrics for needle-turned appliqué should also be 100% cotton, to make your stitching easier. Avoid fabrics that have a heavily-printed design that creates an almost painted surface, as these are hard to stitch through. For my first pieces of hand appliqué I chose a plain cream background fabric; the illustrations I'd seen of original Baltimore Album quilts made me think that plain fabric was necessary to show off the appliqué. Then I started to use

## Pins

◇ Choose short, sharp, fine pins with smooth heads.

## Scissors

◇ Small, sharp-to–the-point scissors are essential for accurate cutting. With blunt scissors it's easy to exert too much pressure and cut too far …

◇ Small, sharp paper scissors with pointed blades help you to achieve accurate templates. Your final appliqué shape can only be as good as the template you cut!

## Rotary-cutting equipment

◇ A cutting mat, ruler and rotary-cutter make cutting bias strips, blocks and borders much easier and more accurate.

◇ A 15in square ruler is useful for cutting background squares and for squaring up blocks when they are finished.

## Markers/drawing equipment

◇ You will need a well-sharpened pencil for tracing shapes accurately.

◇ A removable marker for marking round templates on fabric. There are various types and brands on the market, but choose one which gives a fine, accurate line. Clover™ white marking pen (fine) is one example – the line disappears with the use of the iron or water. Another type is a ceramic lead pencil which comes with replaceable leads in several colours; the line is removed with an eraser or water.

◇ A Pigma Micron 01 pen is useful for inking details on fabric and making labels. It's also good for tracing overlays (more later; see p12).

◇ A *hera* (a Japanese marking tool) is useful for marking quilting lines; the hera leaves a sharp crease on the fabric, so there are no lines to erase.

## Supplies for template making

◇ Freezer paper makes ideal templates which can be re-used many times before they lose their adhesive properties.

◇ A circle template is invaluable for drawing circles on fabric as well as for making card templates. You can generally find this kind of template in art shops and stationers'.

◇ Pre-cut Mylar circles (see p20) are wonderful for making perfect circles for berries, grapes, cherries etc. Mylar™ is a heat-resistant plastic; don't confuse it with ordinary template plastic, which distorts when heat is applied. (This is an important point as the fabric is gathered over the circle and then pressed with a hot iron.) You could of course make your own card circles for templates, but it is quite difficult to cut tiny, accurate, smooth circles!

## Bias Bars

◇ These are narrow bars, usually made of plastic but also sometimes metal, available in various widths; bias bars are used to make narrow tubes of fabric for stems, vines and baskets (see p28). Plastic electrical ties make a good alternative!

◇ Bias maker. This useful gadget is used to fold and press bias strips to make bias binding, which can then be used for various purposes such as creating trailing vines and woven baskets. Bias makers are available in different widths – I find the ¼in size the most useful (see p29).

## Pressing equipment

◇ A small travel iron or the Clover™ Mini Iron is useful for ironing on templates and pressing small areas.

◇ A Teflon pressing sheet or baking sheet can be used to protect your work when you are giving it a final press; it's also useful to protect the ironing board and iron when using fusible web. (Baking parchment serves a similar purpose.)

## Getting a good view – light and magnifier

Good light is essential for good stitching. Natural daylight is best for colour-matching, but even in this it's helpful to have additional lighting for detailed stitching. A light that simulates daylight, and which can be angled to the correct position for you, is the most useful; some lights also incorporate a magnifier, which is even better. I find that a magnifier enables me to sew more quickly, with greater accuracy and less eye strain; it's worth trying one to see if it helps you too. If you don't have a light with a magnifier, use a separate magnifying lens that either stands on the table or is clamped to the edge of the table; once again choose one with a flexible arm so that it too can be angled for the best position. It's also possible to fix a small magnifier to some models of sewing machine. I use my normal magnifier, clamped to the table and angled so I look through it, while I'm machining intricate raw-edge appliqué. If you feel that your eyesight could do with a boost, and there isn't a magnifier available for your machine, you could try this technique too.

## Threads

My preferred thread for hand appliqué is YLI™ #100 silk thread, as it's very fine and comes in a wide range of colours. If you're just beginning appliqué, start with a couple of basic neutral colours in a dark and a medium shade, as these will blend in with many fabrics. One or two green threads will also be useful: #221 works well on dark and medium greens, and #219 on medium and light greens. Build up your collection with different colours as the need arises. When you're choosing thread colour, rather than placing the reel on the fabric, pull out a length from the reel and place it on the fabric; as the thread is so fine, you'll be surprised how one thread colour will blend with many different-coloured fabrics. Although the silk thread is a little more expensive than other threads, it's worth it in the end for the quality of stitching you can achieve. Also, when you're hand appliquéing you use very little thread, so the 200m reel will last you forever as long as you don't lose it!

Silk is easy to sew with by hand if you bear the following tips in mind:

◇ Cut a length of thread roughly the distance from your fingertip to elbow.

◇ Run the thread across beeswax to prevent it from tangling while you're stitching.

◇ To overcome problems of the needle becoming unthreaded, tie the thread in the needle (see sequence a-e). The thread is so fine that the knot passes easily through the fabric.

a  Loop the short end of the thread over itself.

b  Insert the needle through the loop.

c  Pull the loop over the eye of the needle.

d  Pull the short end of the thread to tighten the knot.

e  Pull the long end of the thread to bring the knot up to the eye of the needle.

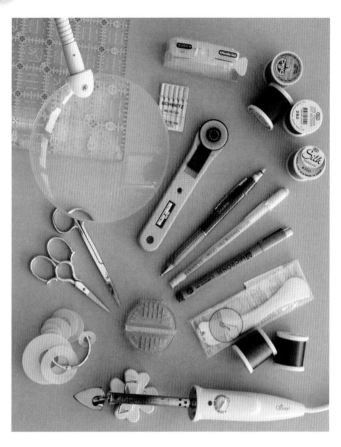

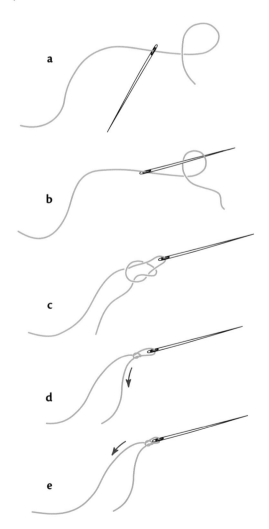

The silk thread has other uses besides hand appliqué. It works very well for machined raw-edge appliqué – particularly using a straight stitch to sew around small pieces on detailed designs. It also works well for beautiful detailed free machine quilting and small-scale quilted background grids (see *Robin Wreath* version 2 on p87); use a fine cotton thread in the bobbin.

Alternatives to the #100 silk thread are fine cotton threads: one example is DMC™ #50 machine embroidery thread.

## *Organisation*

Finally, organizing your equipment and working area will be time well spent, and also avoid the frustration of looking for missing things! Appliqué generally involves handling lots of small pieces of fabric, so it pays to keep them organized in some way. The system I use is to keep all the chosen fabrics in a small basket together with a folder containing all the templates and the full-size design. While I'm stitching I keep a small box beside me into which I can drop the templates as they are finished with – these can later be stored in a large envelope labelled with the name of the design. Remember that freezer paper templates can be used many times. I also keep a shallow tray beside me on which I have my turning stick, small pin-cushion, small scissors, beeswax, needle-case, marking pens and the threads I am using for that particular project. This way, everything I'm using is kept close at hand and I don't have to hunt for things.

# *How to position appliqué*

Usually it's helpful to have the centre lines marked on the background fabric. Fold the fabric in half vertically and lightly finger-press the fold. (Don't iron the centre lines, otherwise you'll find it difficult to remove them later.) Mark the crease with small tacking stitches in a coloured thread (not too dark, so that it doesn't shed dark fibres on the work). Fold the fabric in half the other way, matching the two halves of the tacked line, and finger-press; mark the creased line with tacking as before. If you're working on a very simple design, on which you're just positioning the pieces 'by eye,' you might find that finger-pressing alone is enough; however, if you're using an overlay it is advisable to tack the lines so you can see them easily through the overlay.

There are various ways to position the appliqué shapes on the background. Here are three that I use at different times, depending on the complexity of the design.

◇ Use a light-box: this is a quick method for very simple designs. Tape the design on the top of the light-box, then place the background fabric on top, matching the centre lines marked on the fabric with the centre lines of the design. Tape the corners of the fabric down to prevent any shifting. Position and then pin the appliqué pieces in place using the design as a guide.

a

◇ Tracing the design is another option: use a light-box if you can't see through the background fabric. Match the centre lines of the fabric and the design, and tape the design and background to the work surface for accurate placement. Using a sharp pencil (or white marker on dark fabrics), trace the design onto the right side of the background fabric. I only use this method for stems, or for marking some placement dots for leaves, pots etc on a very simple design such as *Midnight Dance* (**a**); generally an overlay works better, for the reasons mentioned below.

◇ Use an overlay to position the appliqué accurately on the background – this saves having to mark the design on the background. An overlay is very useful for multi-layered appliqué designs; if you draw the full design on the background, any interior design lines are hidden as soon as you have stitched down the first layer. Using an overlay, though, means that the outline of the design is always visible – and also there are no marking lines to remove should your appliqué not quite cover them!

## How to make an overlay

I use a lightweight interfacing onto which the design can be traced; check carefully, though, as many interfacings have built-in stretch and are too soft. You need a reasonably crisp but see-through type (see *Resources* on p128).

**1** Cut a piece of overlay fabric about 2in larger all round than the actual design. Tape the design onto your work surface; position the interfacing on top, and tape the corners to the work surface to prevent movement while you're tracing the design. With a Pigma micron 0.1 pen, trace the design (including the centre lines) onto the interfacing.

TIP: It's a good idea to mark TOP at the top of the overlay. You won't make the mistake then of reversing the overlay when you come to attach it to the background fabric.

**2** On a flat surface, position the overlay on the prepared background fabric so that the centre lines match. Pin the centre, then the ends of the centre lines, and finally the top edge, keeping everything smooth and flat (**b**). Now work a running stitch along the top edge to secure the overlay to the background. Fasten your thread on and off very firmly so that the overlay doesn't work loose while you are working on the project.

When you are not using the overlay to position shapes it can be rolled up and pinned at the top of the work.

*How to position appliqué*

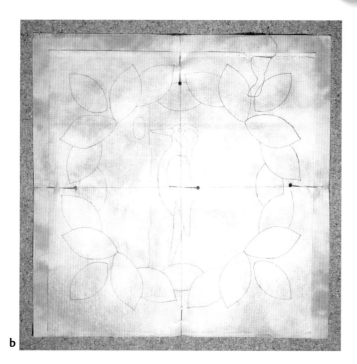

b

**3** If you're doing a design that includes complex flowers and birds, for instance *Robin Wreath* on p80 (detail shown in **c**), it's very useful to make a separate, clear plastic overlay to help you place the pieces accurately as you pre-assemble the complex units. When you're creating a flower, there's some leeway with the petal placement; the flower will still look beautiful. But bird parts need to be accurately assembled if the poor thing isn't to finish up with a droopy undercarriage or a crooked tail! To make a plastic overlay, trace the bird or flower onto a piece of clear, lightweight plastic (eg the clear sheets used for OHP/photocopier transparencies, or packaging plastic); use a fine marker suitable for drawing/writing on plastic (**d**). A clear plastic overlay like this is also useful for selecting particular parts of shaded fabric for the different appliqué shapes (**e**).

c

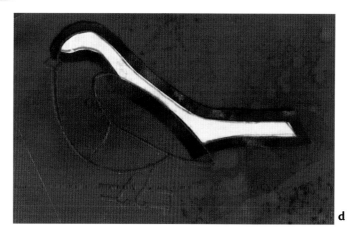

d

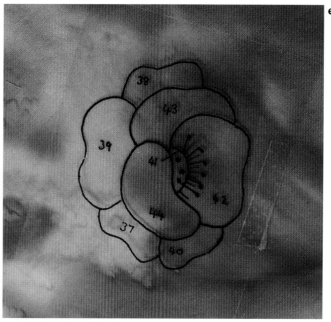

e

## Alternative overlay materials

Tracing paper can be used for an overlay but it is not very durable; you might find it useful for a simple quick design. I used paper overlays for the daisy units in the *Daisy Meadow* project (see p100). If you prefer, instead of using interfacing for the main overlay you can use thin, clear plastic. The design can be photocopied onto a photocopy transparency; you may need to copy the design in sections and then stick the sections together with clear tape to make the full overlay.

Obviously this type of overlay is not so portable, as it can't be rolled up like an interfacing overlay, but it is quick and accurate to produce and use – and of course if you are reducing or enlarging a design you can do both steps in one. Also, if you need to reverse a design for fused appliqué, you can turn the plastic over to get the reversed image for tracing the shapes onto the fusible web. I tend to mix and match my overlay materials according to the design and situation; generally I use interfacing for the main overlay, and make a plastic overlay for any unit appliqué – pre-assembled units such as birds, complex flowers etc.

# Appliqué techniques

*The projects in the book have been stitched using several different appliqué methods and techniques. In this section you will find detailed instructions and tips for needle-turned hand appliqué and fused raw-edge machined appliqué. I've also included instructions for faced shapes and broderie perse. For each project in the book, the instructions will refer to particular appliqué methods used for that project, but you will also find several suggestions for creating the same project using alternative techniques. If you'd like to try out some of the different appliqué methods, the* Leafy Tree *cushion project (see p30) is a good starter project.*

*In the project instructions, I frequently refer back to this section to avoid repetition. I suggest that you read through this whole section first to familiarise yourself generally with the content, and then refer back as necessary when you need help with a particular technique – for example, how to appliqué perfect circles, or how to 'fussy-cut' fused appliqué. You will find this section a useful reference for any appliqué design.*

*Needle-turned appliqué*

*Raw-edge machine appliqué*

*Dimensional appliqué*

# $\mathcal{B}$asic needle-turning techniques

## Preparation

### Prepare the freezer paper template

**1**   Use a sharp pencil to trace the shape from the design sheet onto the matt side of the freezer paper; number the template, and write the same number beside the template (**a**). When an edge is covered by an adjacent shape it will not need to be turned under; mark any such edges with a dotted line.

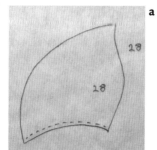

### Make a 'pattern window'

**2**   Carefully cut out the template, leaving a complete hole the exact size of the template which can then be used as a pattern window. (You may prefer to use a small craft knife rather than scissors to cut out templates.) The 'window' is used to help you choose the most effective area of the fabric to use for a particular shape; for example photo **b** shows a leaf template on a good area of a particular fabric as it indicates a central vein. Photo **c** shows the same template positioned on an area of the fabric which doesn't work so well. Leaf prints can be very useful, but make sure that

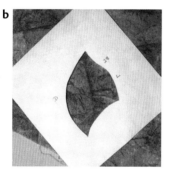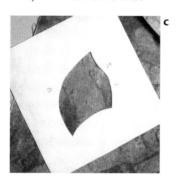

the veins run in the correct direction; if you mark the tip of the leaf on the window and on the template (**d**), this will help you get the direction right. If I'm trying to keep the light falling consistently across the design I mark the light and dark edges on each shape on the design sheet by 'L' and 'D'; you can use the same notation on the templates and windows to avoid confusion (**e**).

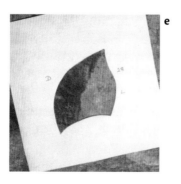

### Prepare the appliqué shapes

**3**   Use the pattern window to select the position for your template. Once you've chosen, drop the template back in the window (**f**), remove the outer window, and iron the template onto the right side of the fabric (**g**); use a hot iron

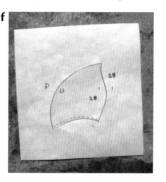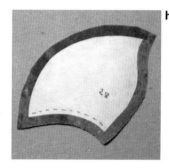

(cotton setting) and a firm surface. Cut out the shape, adding a scant ⅛in seam allowance (**h**). If the fabric tends to fray you could add ¼in and trim back later; on edges which are to be covered by another shape it is also a good idea to add a little more seam allowance in case there is any movement and the raw edge is not quite covered.

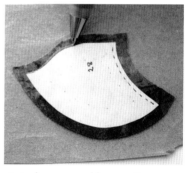

**4**   Use a marking pen (see *Equipment* on p9) to draw round the template shape (**i**). If you place a piece of fine sandpaper under the fabric while you're drawing round the template, it will help keep the fabric flat and stop it shifting. If an edge is to be covered by another appliqué shape, indicate this edge with a dotted line instead of a solid line; it will remind you not to turn under and needle-turn this edge. It's easy to get carried away and sew all round a shape, forgetting that some edges are to be left raw as they'll be covered by other shapes.

· · · · · · · · · · · · · · · · · · · · ·

TIP: A word about grain direction. With small shapes, grain direction is not really an issue – I prefer to 'fussy cut' my shapes as described in step 2 and get the shading I need. Having said that, though, I must also say that bias-cut leaves do needle-turn very well. However, on larger pieces – for example the pot in *Midnight Dance* and the basket base in *Spring Basket* – place the templates on the straight grain of the fabric; matching the grain direction of the appliqué piece to the background in this way will ensure that the shape lies flat and smooth.

· · · · · · · · · · · · · · · · · · · · ·

### Position the shape on the background

**5** Check that the overlay (see p12) is correctly positioned over the design, with the centre lines matching. Slide the prepared shape under the overlay (**j**). Line up the template carefully with the design on the overlay, then hold the shape in place while you fold back the overlay. Place two pins in the seam allowance only to hold the shape in place; pinning through the paper will cause the shape to shift out of position (**k**). Remove the freezer paper and work a line of running stitch ¼in inside the drawn line; finally remove the pins (**l**).

j

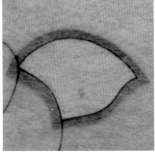

k

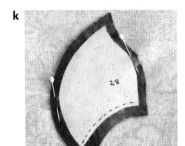

l

## *Perfecting the stitch: ten steps to success!*

**1** Hold the work with the edge to be appliquéd facing away from you. Right-handed stitchers will be stitching from right to left. Start stitching either where the edge is not turned under (if there is one), or at a straighter part of the shape: don't start at a point!

**2** With a knot at the end of the thread, work a small stitch under the shape to get started (**a**).

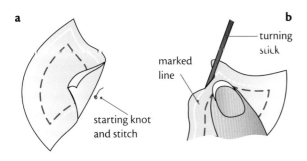

a

b

turning stick

marked line

starting knot and stitch

**3** Stroke under about ¾in of the seam allowance, using either the side of the needle or a small turning stick (**b**). Twist the stick to help roll the edge under so that the marked line is just under the edge; with either the needle or the turning stick you need to make a curving arc action in a counter-clockwise direction, so that any fullness in

the seam allowance is pulled back behind where you are stitching. Firmly finger-press the turned-under edge; frequent finger-pressing helps to 'tame' the turned edge.

**4** Bring needle up through the folded edge (**c**).

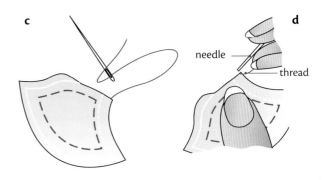

c

d

needle

thread

**5** Keeping the needle perpendicular, insert it into the background against the appliqué edge, opposite the place where the thread emerges from the folded edge (**d**).

**6** Keep the needle almost parallel with the edge as you make a short stitch in the background. Bring the needle up through the background to just catch the opposite fold in the appliqué (**e**); it helps to keep your left thumb just ahead of the needle to hold the edge down.

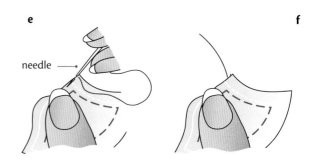

e

f

needle

**7** The length of stitch you take on the background depends on the situation; a complex edge will need shorter stitches than a straight edge or gentle curve. An average size for most situations would be about 12-15 stitches to the inch. Pull the thread away from the edge to help prevent puckering (**f**); this completes the first stitch. Repeat from step 5. After one or two stitches, finger-press the edge to keep it flat and smooth.

**8** As you work your way round the shape, you will need to keep sweeping under the seam allowance as necessary. On fairly straight edges you will be able to turn under about an inch at a time; on curved shapes you will need to make more frequent adjustments to keep a smoothly-curved edge.

**9** Check the back of the work. The stitch should resemble small, straight, close-together running stitches

**10** To fasten off the thread, take the needle through to the back and work a couple of tiny back stitches in the background under the appliqué.

*Appliqué techniques*

## Trouble-shooting

As with all hand skills, your needle-turning technique will improve with practice. Here are a few tips if you are having problems.

### PROBLEM: *the appliquéd edges are uneven*

SOLUTION: this is often the result of too large a gap between the stitches, or it could be that the needle is not re-entering the background directly opposite where it emerges on the appliqué shape. If there are big gaps between the stitches the edge isn't held down sufficiently, which will lead to an uneven edge and possibly fraying at inner curves. Check the back, too – have you missed a stitch and not caught the background? This can cause an uneven edge.

### PROBLEM: *the stitches are visible on the right side, and the edges are uneven*

SOLUTION: check the back. Are your stitches slanting? This happens when you hold the needle in a slanting position as though you're hemming. We're so used to doing hemming stitches that it needs a conscious effort to hold the needle in a different way. Hold the needle in a more upright position as it enters the background, and keep the needle almost parallel with the edge as you make the stitch into the background.

### PROBLEM: *the stitches show on the right side*

SOLUTION: it's not necessary for your stitches to be completely invisible: tiny, even stitches look good too. However, using a fine thread (such as the YLI™ #100 silk thread, see p10) in a toning or exact match helps tremendously. Make sure that you are coming up through the folded edge when you're making each stitch; check too that the stitch doesn't extend beyond the appliqué shape – this leads to 'hairy' edges around the shape!

### PROBLEM: *the stitching puckers*

SOLUTION: you may be pulling the stitches too tight, but what's more likely is that the thread is being pulled backwards after making a stitch. This is the way we're used to sewing, so it's a hard habit to change. Pulling the thread away from the edge at right angles prevents the work puckering. Also, automatically finger-pressing the edge after making a stitch or two helps to keep the edge flat.

### PROBLEM: *'scalloped' edges around the shape*

SOLUTION: you may be bringing the needle up in the appliqué shape too far from the folded edge, and/or inserting the needle too far under the edge, so nipping in the edge and causing a wavy, scalloped effect.

# Curves and Points

## Inner curves

**1** Make a small clip in the seam allowance, cutting almost to the marked line (**a**). Depending on the acuteness of the curve you may need to make several clips (**b**). Swing the edge under with the turning stick; the

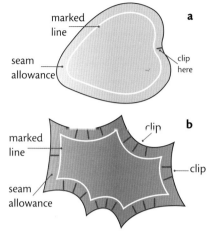

stick works very well on inner curves, and enables you to achieve a smooth edge. If the edge will not turn under sufficiently, make an additional clip, or make the clips slightly deeper – but not past the marked line!

**2** Keep the stitches close together on a clipped edge, to prevent fraying and to ensure a smooth edge around the appliqué shape.

## Outer curves

**1** On outer edges there is no need to make any clips or notches in the seam allowance; the seam allowance is so small that any fullness can be absorbed within the turned edge. If you find that the edge will not turn under smoothly, you can reduce the seam allowance slightly.

**2** I prefer to use the needle rather than the turning stick for turning under outer curves. If necessary on tight curves you can even use the point of the needle to pull the seam allowance under and adjust it into place to achieve a smooth line; do this with care, though, as you don't want to pluck and fray the edge.

**3** Ease the edge under a small amount at a time; this may mean that you will have to adjust the edge every stitch or so on a very tight curve. Keep your thumb just below the curved edge to hold the

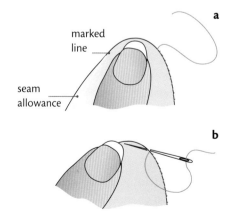

shape in place as you tuck under the curved edge to give a smooth line (**a**). Then slide your thumb up to hold the turned edge in place as you stitch it down (**b**). On tight curves the stitches need to be close and small, so that the edge is well anchored and retains an accurate shape.

## Inner points

**1** You will need to clip the seam allowance at an inner point. Mark the position of the cut with a white marking pen (**a**), or a fine line of clear nail varnish (which also helps to prevent fraying). It's often convenient to mark any cuts when you are preparing the shapes and before tacking them in position – don't actually make the cut though at this stage!

**2** Stitch to about ½in from the inner point. Clip the seam on the marked cut line, clipping to the drawn line of the shape. Use the stick to turn the seam under, and continue stitching towards the base of the inner point (**b**). Keep the stitches small and close – there is only a scant seam allowance.

**3** When you reach the base, turn under the adjacent side of the point, pulling the stick down at the base to create a sharp inner point (**c**). At this stage you may have to clip another thread or two at the base if the edge will not turn under sufficiently.

**4** At the very base of the point you need to take a slightly deeper stitch. Work this stitch in two stages. First, bring the needle up through the appliqué fabric, taking a slightly bigger 'bite 'than usual (**d**). Return the needle into the background, slanting the needle just under the edge a little more than usual. Place your left thumb over the stitch as you pull the thread firmly – this prevents puckering. This slightly bigger stitch will disappear into the fabric and firmly secure the base of the point.

**5** Start stitching up the second side of the point. Work the first two or three stitches in two stages like a stab stitch, so that you don't pluck out the minuscule seam allowance; make the stitches small and close together for great security. Continue stitching as usual after this.

**6** When you are stitching a long inner point, divide the seam allowance evenly between the two edges (**e**).

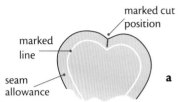
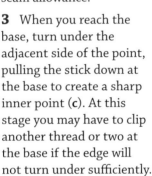
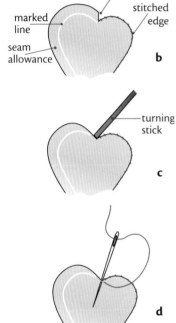
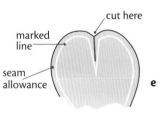

## Outer points

These sometimes make appliqué stitchers anxious, but I think that using the technique below, you will find them easier than tight outer curves. Here are two methods and a few tips to reduce stress levels.

**1** Needle-turn to the point, stopping just before the marked line. Keep the stitching small as you approach the corner, for extra security.

**2** Hold the work firmly between the third and fourth fingers on your left hand, to create a bit of tension on the background fabric.

**3** Pick up the corner on the point of the needle (**a**), and swing the seam allowance under through 180°; the needle will now be pushed firmly against the first line of stitching. Carefully remove the needle and pull gently on the thread to re-align the point which may have loosened in the turning process (**b**). Work a small stitch at the point. It sometimes help at this stage to push the flat end of the turning stick down under the point, to smooth out any seam allowance which may have got bunched up underneath the first side as you were stitching it.

**4** Turn the seam allowance under on the second side of the point, and continue stitching as usual.

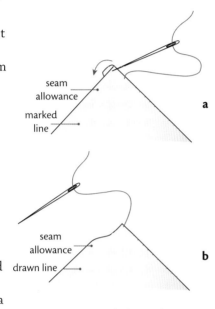

An alternative method for turning points is to use a flat-ended turning stick – most quilters find this method much easier. It's easy to adapt a regular turning stick by whittling the end to produce a flat chisel-type shape.

Begin as described above, up to the end of step 2. Hold the stick as shown and push the point round and under (**c**), flattening the stick against the background as you turn (**d**).

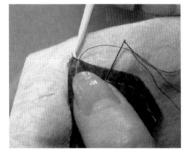
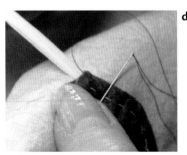

As in the first method, push the stick down inside the point a couple of times to smooth out any turnings which may have got bunched up. Re-align the point as before by pulling the thread, and work a

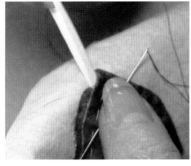
e

small stitch at the point. It's useful to turn under some of the seam allowance along the second side of the point too with the flat end of the stick, before continuing the appliqué (e).

TIP: Sometimes beginners have problems because they have wandered away from the marked line as they approach the point, so that there is very little seam allowance left at the point itself. Try to keep the marked line tucked under, pinning across the shape if necessary near the point.

## Acute outer points

**1**  When you are stitching an acute point, it's useful to remove some of the seam allowance after stitching the first side of the point; doing this reduces bulk and helps create a sharper point. Use small, very sharp-pointed scissors; slide the scissor points under the shape, and trim a sliver off the seam allowance on the stitched edge. A similar technique is helpful when you are stitching very narrow shapes (see *Daisy Meadow* on p102).

**2**  It may be necessary to turn the point in two stages, even if you don't trim the seam allowance. Turn once as shown (**a**), and then again to complete the point (**b**).

a

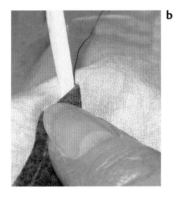
b

# Cut-away appliqué

This is a useful method to choose for a shape which has several narrow stems or branches, for instance a tree silhouette. I used this method for the thin branching stems of the sprig of mistletoe in the *Christmas Heart* design on p92.

**1**  Trace the shape onto freezer paper and cut it out to make a template. Cut a rectangle of fabric a little larger than the template, and iron the template onto the right side of the appliqué fabric, shiny side down (**a**). (The diagrams show a template that I used for the narrow branching stems of a fuchsia.)

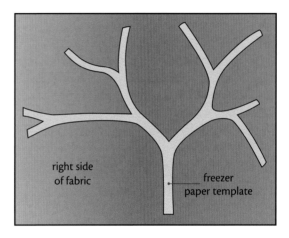

right side of fabric — freezer paper template

a

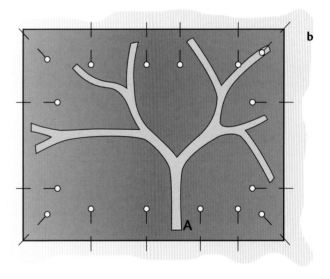

b

A

**2**  Draw round the template as usual. Place the rectangle of appliqué fabric on the background, lining up the template in the usual way with the overlay, and pin in place (**b**). Remove the template and use the drawn line as a guide for needle-turning the edge.

**3**  Tack the appliqué fabric in place. On broader shapes you can use running stitches ¼in inside the drawn line as usual. With narrow shapes (such as these stems) this technique isn't possible, so tack on the opposite edge from where you will begin to needle-turn the shape.

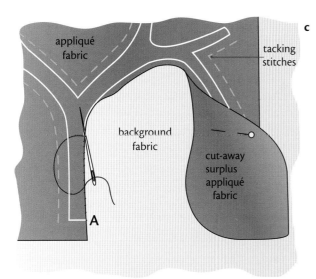

**4** Start at point A and cut away some of the appliqué fabric for a short distance, adding the usual seam allowance. Needle-turn the edge in place until you need to cut a little more of the fabric away. Continue in this way around the shape, trimming back the fabric and stitching small sections; you can pin back the surplus fabric until it's more convenient to cut off a section completely (**c**).

## Perfect circles

**1** Circles feature widely in appliqué, whether that's as flower centres, berries or fruits, so it's useful to be able to appliqué an accurate circle. It helps enormously to use a pre-cut circle; the Mylar™ ones (see *Resources* on p128) come in a variety of sizes (**a**) and are re-usable. Alternatively you can cut your own circle templates from cardboard, but you do need to cut accurately.

**2** Cut the fabric ½in larger in diameter than the finished size. So, for example, for a ¼in finished circle the fabric will need to be cut as a ¾in-diameter circle; a ½in finished circle will need a 1in-diameter fabric circle and so on. A circle template is very useful for helping you to cut accurate fabric circles (**b**).

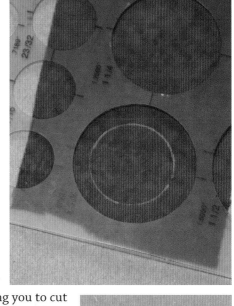

**3** Without securing the thread either at the beginning or at the end of the stitching, work small running stitches ⅛in inside the outer edge of the fabric circle (**c**).

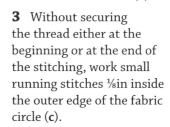

**4** Position the plastic circle centrally on the wrong side of the fabric circle, twist one end of the thread over the other, then hold both ends of the thread and pull them up together tightly (**d**). Press the circle firmly on the back with a hot iron.

**5** Ease back the gathering thread a little so that you can remove the plastic circle – tweezers are useful for this operation. Gently pull up the gathers again to return the fabric to the original shape (**e**).

**6** Appliqué the circle in position using small stitches. Be careful not to pull the stitches too tight and distort the edge. It helps to use a slightly different appliqué stitch to keep the edge smooth. Run the needle under the folded outer edge of the circle, taking a small stitch in the seam allowance before inserting the needle into the background. Take a small stitch in the background before bring the needle back up under the edge of the circle. Continue in this way around the circle, making sure that you keep a smooth outer edge all the way around the shape.

**7**  The seam allowances will pad the shape slightly, but you can push in a little wadding before you complete the appliqué to create extra padding.

**8**  An alternative method for making a smooth circle is to use heavyweight interfacing instead of a plastic or card circle for pressing. Draw a circle in the required finished size on the interfacing. Cut this out and use it instead of the plastic circle as above in steps 2–4 above, but leave the interfacing inside the pressed circle. Some quilters find they can achieve a smoother circle using this method, especially if you adapt your appliqué stitch slightly as explained in step 6.

**9**  The pre-turned circle can also be machined in place with a small zigzag stitch.

## Finally ...

This description of basic needle-turning techniques may sound a little daunting – especially to beginners. I have tried to give lots of detail based on my teaching experience; if you do have problems with the stitch itself, I hope that my suggestions will help you to overcome them. The most important thing, though, is to practise, and not to be disheartened if your first efforts aren't quite as good as you would like. Choose a good-quality fabric, not too thick or loosely-woven, start with a small simple project, and enjoy the learning process!

## *Machined fused raw-edge appliqué*

There are several ways to appliqué by machine – here is the method which I use most frequently, and it will work very well for the projects in the book.

Any basic domestic sewing machine can be used for appliqué, and an open-toed foot (nb, an open-toed *presser* foot, not an open, free-quilting foot) is very helpful for negotiating round intricate shapes. A knee-lift is also extremely helpful when you need to raise the presser foot frequently; this facility, which is available on some machines, enables you to keep your hands free to guide the work, while your knee operates the knee-lift to raise and lower the machine foot.

I like to use the same fine threads that I use for hand appliqué for machine appliqué too. The machine-stitched projects in this book have been stitched with either a straight stitch or a small open zigzag, and for this the fine threads work well. If your machine does a blanket stitch you could use this instead, but on very small, intricate shapes a straight stitch will be easier. Use a #50 cotton thread with the buttonhole stitch – #40 can be used for a bolder effect on larger shapes.

Satin stitch is another alternative for machine appliqué, but this would be too heavy for most of my designs, where the shapes are small and the edge is unobtrusive.

Use a Microtex needle #70, which is a fine, sharp needle and ideal for use with fine threads.

## Fusible web

There are several brands of fusible web available. I prefer to use the lightweight type which sticks shapes temporarily in position when they're finger-pressed firmly, which enables you to arrange the shapes on the background and reposition them if necessary. The web doesn't bond permanently until you apply a warm iron. The instructions I've given below are general instructions for using fusible web: always refer to the specific instructions for your chosen product.

## Preparing templates

**1**  Trace the templates in reverse onto the 'paper' side of the web. (Note that the design for the *Robin Wreath* version 2 on p87 is given in reverse, so on this particular project the templates should be traced directly from the design). Some products have a loose protective paper backing – make sure that you are tracing onto the paper with the adhesive backing! Where shapes overlap, mark the underneath edge with a dotted line (**a**).

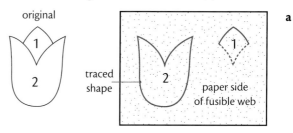

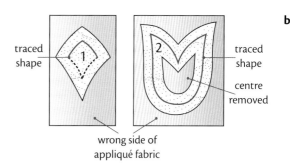

**2**  Cut out each shape, adding a ¼in seam allowance. On all but the very smallest shapes, cut out the centre of the template ¼in inside the traced line, as shown on template 2 in the diagram; removing the centre means the final appliqué piece is softer. This is especially true on large shapes, which can be very stiff if the whole shape is bonded to the background. Iron the templates onto the back of your chosen appliqué fabric (**b**), adhesive side against the fabric.

You may want to 'fussy-cut' the shape, but it's not quite so easy to do this when you are working in reverse on the back of the fabric. However it is possible to use freezer paper 'windows' (see p15) to identify your chosen area on the right side of the fabric; iron the window in position on the right side, then push pins through to indicate where you should put the fusible web shape on the back of the fabric. This is a fairly accurate method, but if you want to get the shading exactly right, work on a light-box. Once you've ironed the freezer paper window in place on the right side as described above, place the fabric right side down on a light-box; the silhouette of the freezer paper will show through, and you can match the drawn line on the template with the outline of the window, then iron it in place on the wrong side of the fabric. Either way I know it's a little extra work, but worth it if you want to get a particular shading – for example, as I've done for the robin and leaves in the fused version of *Robin Wreath* on p87.

**3**  Cut out the shape on the traced line. As you will be cutting through the fusible web and the fabric, this ensures that the fusible web is covering the complete edge of the shape (**c**). Where shapes meet, add a ¹⁄₁₆in extra on the edge that you marked with a dotted line on the shape that goes underneath (**d**); that will then create a slight overlap when you position the shapes, and avoid any gaps between them. Remove the paper backing from the shapes.

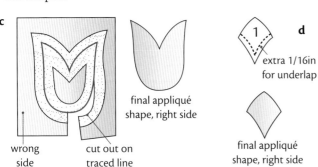

c

wrong side

cut out on traced line

final appliqué shape, right side

1

extra 1/16in for underlap

d

final appliqué shape, right side

- - - - - - - - - - - - - - - - - - - - - - - - - - - -

TIP: Use a pressing sheet (see *Equipment* on p9) or non-stick baking paper to protect your iron and ironing board when you're using fusible web! Place the sheet both under and over the work.

- - - - - - - - - - - - - - - - - - - - - - - - - - - -

## Positioning the appliqué

**1**  Position the appliqué shape on the background using one of the methods described on p12. Working with the design on a light-box can work well with fused designs: simply tape the design to the light-box, then centre the fabric on top and tape it in position. For the *Robin Wreath*

version 2 (p87) I traced the whole design onto clear plastic and then turned it over to use as an overlay. (Remember that this design is reversed in the book!)

**2**  Press with a hot iron to fuse the shapes permanently in place. Don't move the iron back and forth, or you may move the shapes out of position. (Always double-check the manufacturer's instructions before fusing the shapes in position.)

## Choice of stitch

Stitch with the appliqué shape to the left of the needle. Either stitch around the shape close to the edge, using a small straight stitch, or use a small open zigzag stitch to cover the raw edge. Settings vary on different machines, so try out the width and length settings on a sample before starting a project. On my machine I use length 0.5, width 1; this gives me a stitch which will cover the raw edge (**e**) but is not too heavy and dense (**f**). The scale is also appropriate for the size of the appliqué shapes I have used in these projects. However, on larger shapes you could use a wider stitch. For appliqué on children's quilts,

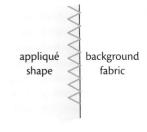

e

appliqué shape

background fabric

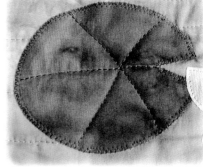

f

and other items that will be subjected to frequent washing, I would use a closer and wider zigzag stitch to produce a stronger finish. Whichever stitch you choose, do remember to hold the thread behind the presser foot as you begin to machine so that the thread doesn't get caught in the stitching.

## Stitching techniques using zigzag stitch

On the diagrams I've used to illustrate these tips, I've enlarged the scale considerably so that you can see what's going on clearly.

Your aim is to cover all the outside edges of the appliqué shape with a continuous zigzag stitch: points and corners therefore need extra care, to ensure that they are completely covered by the stitching. Always stop with the needle down on the outside edge of the shape when you're lifting the presser foot to change direction; you may be able to adjust the speed of your machine, too, which will help when stitching small shapes and intricate edges. With practice, though, it is possible to learn to control the speed so you can stitch a stitch at a time if necessary.

## Curves

Stitch with the appliqué shape to the left of the needle. To negotiate curves you may need to stop several times and re-adjust the fabric to keep a smooth edge; when you need to do this, always stop with the needle down in the work on the outside edge of the shape – that is, with the needle to the right, in the background fabric. Raise the presser foot and pivot the work on the needle to the new position. You may have a 'stop with needle down' facility on your machine which is very useful: if not, use the hand wheel. Lower the presser foot and continue stitching Tight curves and circles will need frequent stops and pivoting to ensure a smooth outer edge; a knee-lift is a great asset here!

## Corners

Stitch up to the corner and stop with the needle on the right (**a**), in the background. Raise the presser foot; turn the work, pivoting on the needle; lower the presser foot, and start stitching again. On the corner the stitching will overlap as shown (**b**).

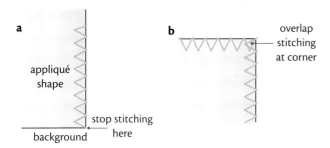

## Outer points

Stitch up to the point, stopping with the needle to the right in the background fabric (**a**). Raise the presser foot and pivot the work slightly. Lower the foot again and take one stitch to the left, on the outside of the previously stitched edge (**b**). Raise the presser foot and pivot the work again so that the next stitch will swing to the outer edge of the appliqué (**c**); the stitching will overlap at the point as shown. Continue stitching down this edge.

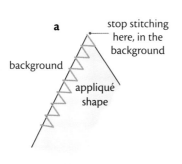

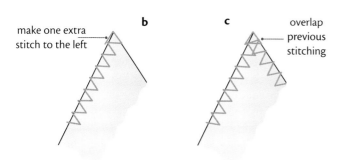

## Inner points

Stop at the base of the point with the needle to the right. Pivot the work slightly to create a stitch to the left into the appliqué (**a**). Pivot slightly again and work another stitch over this first stitch, bringing the needle back into the background. You may need to hold the fabric firmly (to pull it back slightly from feeding under the machine foot) in order to get these stitches in the correct position as shown (**b**).

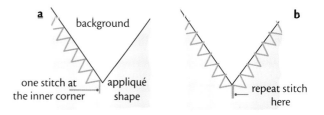

## Fastening off ends

It's a good idea to fasten off the ends as you go along, to prevent a complete 'bird's nest' of tangled threads on the back. Stop sewing after the first few stitches, and pull on the starting thread to bring the bobbin thread up in a loop; pull the loop through, so that both start ends are now on the front of the fabric and can be kept out of the way. At the end of the stitching line, after you've taken the work from the machine, pull on the bobbin thread to bring the top thread through to the back. Tie ends together; these ends can then be threaded in a needle and woven through a few stitches on the back before cutting off. A self-threading needle is helpful!

TIP: A useful way to pull ends through to the back is to use a needle threaded as shown with a loop of strong thread (a); this method saves a lot of time when machine quilting. Thread a loose end into the loop and use the needle to pull it through to the back of the work (b).

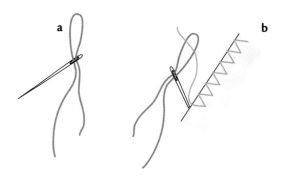

If the work is already layered as a quilt sandwich (see p122), tie the top and bottom ends together on the back, place them in the thread loop and weave the needle through the wadding for a couple of inches to bury the ends – then cut them off. This method also works if the ends are too short to be threaded in a needle and taken through to the back.

## More appliqué techniques

There are many other appliqué techniques that will enhance your work, and here are two more that I find particularly useful. Faced appliqué is good for creating dimensional elements in a design, and broderie perse is a perfect method for appliquéing printed motifs.

### Faced shapes

I've used this method in several of the projects, for instance the fence on the *Sunflowers and Butterflies* design (p62), some of the leaves and flowers on the *Cyclamen Pot* (p70), and some of the lily leaves on the *Lily Pond* project (p45). The shapes are made from two layers of fabric, seamed and turned out, so it's a useful method for dimensional shapes which are only partially stitched to the background. Note that, unless you're working with a symmetrical shape that is totally reversible, any templates you're using for this method will need to be reversed.

**1** Make a freezer paper template of the required shape and iron it onto the wrong side of the top fabric. Don't cut the shape out at this stage; it's easier to cut out a small shape after it's been machined.

**2** Put the top fabric and the backing fabric right sides together; pin the two fabrics together (but not through the template), and machine around the edge of the template (**a**).

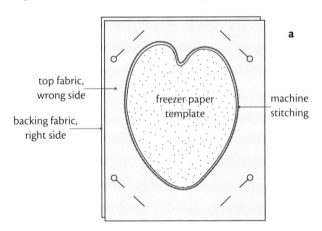

Use a short machine stitch to give you a stronger seam, as the seam allowance will be cut very small. (Alternatively you can draw round shape, remove the template and use the drawn line as a guide for stitching.)

**3** Remove the template. (Save these templates, as they can be re-used). Cut out the shape, leaving a scant ⅛in seam allowance (**b**). Trim any corners; very acute inner curves may need to be clipped, but as the seam allowance is so small no

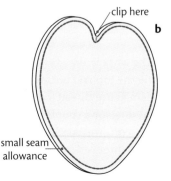

other clipping is necessary. Make a small cut in the centre of the backing fabric (the underside of the finished shape) as shown (**c**); ensure that you only cut through that one layer of fabric and not both layers, so use a pin to help separate the layers before cutting.

**4** Turn the shape right side out through the cut slit; roll the seam out between your fingers to produce a flat edge, and press the shape. Turning the shape through a slit in the back creates a smoother edge on curved shapes than the method explained below.

If the shape has a straight edge, it is possible to leave a gap on this straight edge for turning the shape through to the right side. I used this method to make the fence posts in the *Sunflower* project (p62). When you're cutting out the stitched shape, though, keep a ¼in seam allowance at the gap (**d**) – this will make it easier to fold in the seam allowances on the shape once you've turned it out. Turn the shape to the right side and press, then close the gap with a slip stitch.

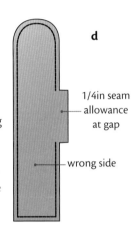

### Broderie perse

Broderie perse involves cutting out motifs from printed fabric and then using these as part of an appliqué design. In the past it was a way of making expensive printed chintz

fabrics go further; the motifs were cut out, either adding a small seam allowance and needle-turning the edge in place, or the raw edges were secured with tiny blanket stitches. Today we have the advantage of being able to use fusible web to attach the motifs to the background. You can stitch the edges by hand, using a blanket stitch, or machine them using the technique described earlier for fused appliqué (p21). Alternatively, you can cut the motifs out adding a small seam allowance, and needle-turn them in the usual way; the photograph above shows a needle-turned broderie perse butterfly.

a

b

For the centre of this cushion design (**a**), I cut flowers from the floral print shown (**b**) and then re-arranged them, adding small blue circles and some embroidery. I fused the shapes in place, and worked a small, close blanket stitch over the raw edges. Groups of small flowers were cut out as a unit and fused in place. It helps if the background colour of the broderie perse fabric matches the colour of the background of your work; then any tiny bits left unstitched between groups of flowers will blend in with the background fabric (**c**).

c

For broderie perse appliqué, look for fabrics with motifs which don't overlap too much. You can usually find suitable flower and leaf prints, as well as butterflies, insects and animals, as shown below. Today, novelty fabrics are available printed with just about every motif you could wish to include in your appliqué!

### Preparing fused shapes

These are the steps I used to prepare one of the pansies from the fabric shown in the photo (**a**). You need to work from the wrong side of the printed fabric, so that your chosen motif will be reversed; use a light-box if you can't easily see the motif on the back of the fabric.

a

**1** Trace the outline of your chosen motif (from the wrong side of the fabric) onto the paper side of a piece of fusible web (**b**).

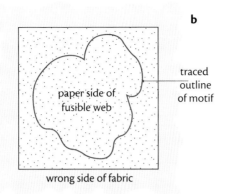

**b**

paper side of fusible web

traced outline of motif

wrong side of fabric

**2** Cut out the fusible web shape, adding ¼in extra all the way round (**c**).

**3** Cut out the centre of the shape about ¼in inside the traced line (**d**). This step isn't necessary on small shapes, but on larger shapes, removing the centre retains the softness of the appliqué shape.

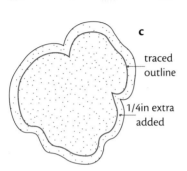

**c**

traced outline

1/4in extra added

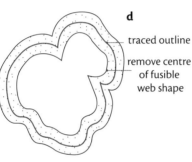

**d**

traced outline

remove centre of fusible web shape

**4** With the paper side uppermost, re-position the fusible web shape on the wrong side of your chosen fabric motif (**e**) – again, you might need to use a light-box. Fuse the fusible web in place, working on a firm surface.

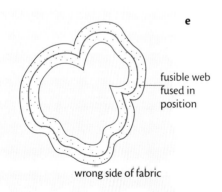

**e**

fusible web fused in position

wrong side of fabric

**5** Working on the right side of the fabric, cut out the chosen motif; cutting out on the right side means that you can follow the shape of the motif exactly. You will be cutting through both the fusible web and fabric, which will give you better a better seal when you fuse the motif to the background. The diagram (**f**) shows the back of the cut-out motif.

### Stitching the shapes

**7** Remove the paper backings, and arrange the shapes in a pleasing design on the background fabric. Once you're happy with the positioning, fuse the shapes in place with a hot iron.

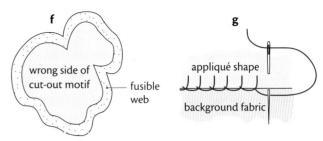

**f**

wrong side of cut-out motif

fusible web

**g**

appliqué shape

background fabric

**8** Either machine the raw edges with a small zigzag, or cover them with blanket stitch (**g**) – in this diagram the stitch is shown enlarged for clarity. I use one strand of matching embroidery thread, and work the stitches close together, making each stitch about ¹⁄₁₆in long. However, depending on the size of the shape and the finished style you want, you could use bolder stitches, larger and spaced further apart.

**8** You can add extra surface embroidery to define details, and quilting can also be used to add definition to individual petals (**h**).

**h**

## Take a bias strip: five ways to make stems

There are several different ways to make stems, and the method you choose depends on the situation. Do you need a very fine stem, a tapered stem, or perhaps a long continuous vine stem? Maybe you want to make twining stems, or to make a woven basket. Read through the instructions and suggestions to help you decide which method to use; perhaps you might like to make samples so that you can compare the techniques. Stems should always be cut on the bias (45° to the straight grain of the fabric); the bias of the fabric (**a**) has the most stretch, so this will enable the stems to curve gracefully and lie smoothly on the background.

**a**

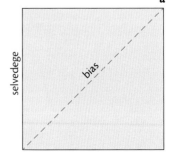

selvedge

bias

The easiest way to cut bias strips of fabric is using a rotary cutter on a cutting mat marked with a 45° line. Lay the fabric on the mat with the straight grain lined up with a horizontal or vertical line on the mat and the fabric covering the 45° line; using a quilt rule and rotary cutter, make a cut on the 45° line (**b**). Use the quilt rule to measure the required width of the stem strip from the cut edge, and cut again (**c**).

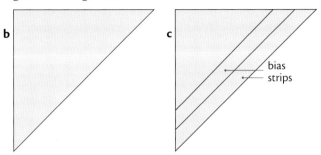

If you need to join the bias strips, join them on the straight grain using a crossway seam (see the *Finishing Touches* section on p124).

These are the five stem methods which I find most useful.

## Method 1

This is the simplest method, and is useful if you have to make very long stems – for example, a trailing vine. I used this method for making the machined stems in the *Sunflowers and Butterflies* panel (p62).

**1**   Cut a 1in-wide bias strip, then fold down a third of the width to the wrong side as shown (**a**). Make the second fold as shown (**b**), and tack down the centre of the strip to hold the layers together. Using this method a 1in bias strip makes

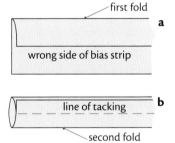

quite a bold stem; for a narrower stem, cut a ¾in bias strip. Store lengths of prepared stems by wrapping them around a cardboard roll.

**2**   You can stitch the stem in place using hand appliqué, or zigzag by machine down each side.

## Method 2 (fine stem method)

This method makes a well-padded, fine stem which is suitable for most hand appliqué designs. The bias strip is generally cut between ¾in and 1in wide; if you want to make a really fine stem, stitch nearer the fold in Step 5 below, and trim back the seam allowance to complete Step 6.

**1**   Fold the strip in half, wrong sides together, and finger-press along its length.

**2**   Only one side of the stem needs to be marked on the background – usually the outer curve. Place the cut edges against the marked line, with the cut edges to the left and

the folded edge on the right. Pin the stem, placing the pins at right angles to the edge (**a**). On outer curves it's advisable to ease the strip a little when you're pinning it in place, so that the stem lies flat after the final stitching. This is particular necessary when you're stitching a stem into a circle; if the stem is too tight it will cause the background to 'puff up' in the centre of the circle.

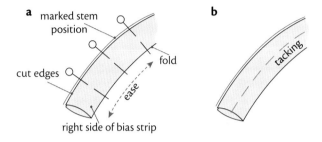

**3**   Mark the centre of the strip with a few dots for guidance if necessary, and tack down the centre line (**b**).

**4**   Stitch the stem with small running stitches, just above the centre dots and nearer the cut edge (**c**). There is a reason for not stitching exactly along the centre. If you stitch exactly in the centre you will find the strip will not cover the drawn line when it's folded over at the next stage.

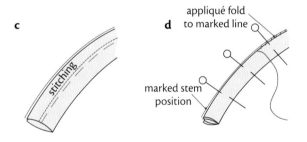

**5**   Remove the tacking. Fold the folded edge over the raw edges and pin at right angles, pinning from the folded edge (**d**); appliqué the folded edge in place.

## Method 3 (alternative fine stem method)

This is my preferred option for a fine stem for three reasons: the first row of stitching fixes the stem correctly in position; the stem can be tapered; and it's possible to make ultra-fine stems

**1**   Cut the bias strip between ¾in and 1in wide. Fold the strip in half, wrong sides together, and finger-press.

**2**   Mark the outer edge of the stem on the background. Place the strip over the stem

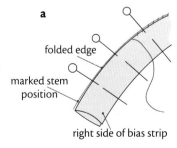

position, with the folded edge of the strip against the drawn line; appliqué the folded edge in position (**a**).

**3** Lift up the top layer of the stem, and trim the underneath layer to leave a little less than half the width (**b**). Turn the top layer of the stem under the trimmed layer, and pin it in place at right angles (**c**). Appliqué the second side of the stem in position.

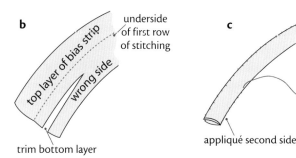

**4** To taper the stem width: after you've stitched the first side, trim the underneath layer as shown (**d**). If you are tapering the stem to a very narrow width, you will need to trim a little off the top layer too before you stitch the second side (**e**). Tweezers are helpful for turning the seam allowances under as you stitch the second side of a very fine stem.

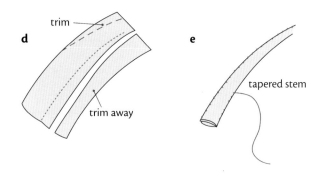

## Method 4 (bias bars)

This method uses bias bars for pressing machine-stitched bias strips, and is very good for creating twining, twisted stems as well as for Celtic designs. I used this method to make the strips for the cyclamen jardinière on p70, as I needed very fine finished strips and I also wanted to be able to weave them. Bias bars (**a**) are usually sold in packs containing various sizes – usually ⅛-½in wide; the most

widely available ones are made of plastic, but sometimes you can find metal bias bars. Some of the bars are a little thick, which makes the finished stem wider than the size of the bar you've used for pressing it; experiment to find the best width of bar to use for a particular project. A very good substitute for bought bias bars is to use electrical ties – these come in various lengths and widths, and you can find them in DIY stores. You may need to search for the longer lengths, as you need ties that are about 10in long. These ties are made from a thinner plastic than some of the 'proper' bias bars, which means the finished pressed strip is nearer the size of the original bar.

**1** Cut the width of the bias strip according to the width of bar you are using. For a bar ¼in wide or less, cut the strip 1in wide; a ⅜in bar will need a strip 1¼in wide. Fold the strip in half, wrong sides facing.

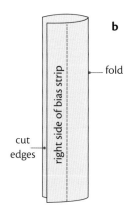

**2** Use a short machine stitch and a contrasting sewing thread – when you can see the stitching it makes the trimming stage easier later on. With the fold on the right, machine a seam to form a channel wide enough for the bar to fit inside snugly (**b**). For example, if you're using a ¼in bar, stitch slightly more than ¼in away from the fold. It's advisable to stitch a few inches, raise the presser foot, and slide the bar into the channel to check the fit; it needs to be snug, but still allow the fabric to slide along the bar. If necessary change the needle position to get the exact fit required.

**3** Once you've stitched the whole length of the strip, push the bar inside the stitched channel and twist the seam so that it lies slightly to the back (**c**). Trim the seam close to the stitching (**d**); I find this easier to do while the bar is in the strip, but you could trim the seam before putting the bar inside. The seam allowance must not

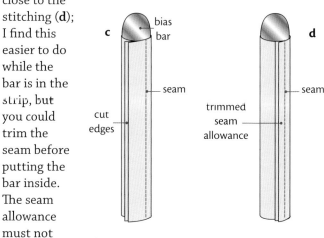

extend beyond the edge of the strip. Working on a firm surface, press the seam to one side, then slide the strip off the bar and press it firmly again to get a crisp finish. If the bias strip is longer than the bar, move the strip along the bar to press the next section.

*Appliqué techniques*

**4** To make a very fine stem, cut the fabric 1in wide and machine the channel to fit a very fine bar (**e**). Twist the seam very slightly to the back and press the strip on the bar (**f**) before trimming closely (**g**); the seam allowance is very tiny and it will be difficult to press after trimming.

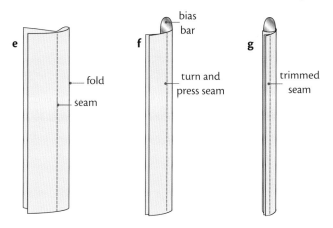

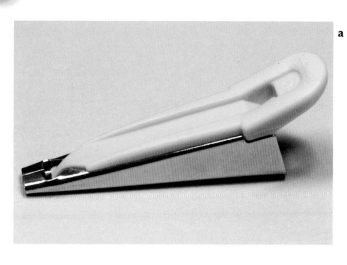

## Method 5 (bias maker)

A bias maker is a useful little gadget for making folded strips similar to purchased bias binding. Bias makers are available in different widths – the ¼in (**a**) is the most useful size for making continuous vines, and strips for woven baskets. Lightly spray-starch and press the fabric before cutting the bias strips, to give them a bit of extra 'body.' Refer to the instructions with your particular bias maker for guidance, but I find that strips cut ⅝in wide work best with a ¼in bias maker, as the cut edges meet better.

I mainly use the bias maker for making fabric strips for woven baskets, as in the *Spring Basket* project (see p112); the specific instructions under that project include further information on using a bias maker.

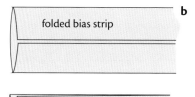

The folded strips made with a bias maker are also an easy way to create fine stems; simply fold each strip again and press it to make a narrower strip (**b** and **c**).

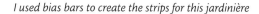

*I used bias bars to create the strips for this jardinière*

*These strips were created with a bias maker*

# Project 1

# A Leafy Tree

*This is a good starter project for your appliqué journey. Why not try some of the methods described in Appliqué Techniques (p14-24) to stitch these simple leaf shapes? Or, if you prefer, needle-turn all the leaves to perfect your stitch and to practise curves and points. In the original I needle-turned most of the leaves except for three, which were cut from a silky polyester fabric. This fabric would have been very difficult to needle-turn, so I used the fused appliqué technique and finished the edge with a small zigzag (p23). I made the three fallen dimensional leaves using the faced shape technique (see p24). You only need small pieces of fabric for the leaves, so have fun choosing fabrics and colours to create either a summer or autumn tree – or, as in my example, you could choose colours to co-ordinate with the colour-scheme of a particular room.*

*Here I've made the design into a cushion cover, but if you prefer to use it as a wall-hanging, add a wider border and more quilting.*

**Finished size:** *The cushion cover measures approx 16in square*

## What you will need

- ½yd for the background fabric and cushion back
- appliqué fabrics:
- for the leaves, small pieces of fabrics in colours of your choice. Choose cotton fabrics for needle-turned leaves, but you could use other fabrics for any fused leaves
- for the tree trunk, one piece 8 x 5in
- for the inner border, four 1 x 15¼in strips
- for the outer border, two 15¼ x 1¼in strips and two 16¾ x 1¼in strips
- silk thread or alternative fine thread to match the appliqué fabrics
- freezer paper for making templates
- for quilting the cushion front:
- stranded embroidery thread for bold quilting
- regular machining thread for subtle quilting
- 18in square low loft wadding
- 18in square backing fabric
- three small buttons to fasten the cushion cover

As this is a beginners' appliqué project, I've included lots of reminders as well as references back to detailed instructions in the *Techniques* section.

## Preparation

**1** Cut a 16in square of background fabric, and mark the centre lines with tacking (see p12).

**2** Make an overlay and attach it (see p12); alternatively, as this is a simple design, you could use the light-box method (see p12), particularly if you intend to fuse most of the design.

**3** Check through your chosen fabric scraps, and plan how you will place the different fabrics. It may help to stick a small snippet of the chosen fabric on each leaf on the design to achieve a balanced effect.

*Steps 4–7 below refer to needle-turned appliqué; if you prefer to fuse the trunk and any of the leaves in place, refer back to the instructions on p21 and then continue from step 8.*

**4** Trace the tree trunk template onto the matt side of the freezer paper; cut out the template, leaving the background intact, to create a pattern window (**a**). Move this over the fabric to view and

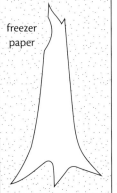
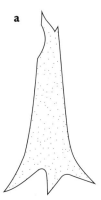

select the best patterning on the fabric for the trunk. (If your chosen fabric doesn't have any particular shading for 'fussy-cutting,' dispense with the window and simply place the template on the right side of the fabric, on the straight grain.) It's best to place the template on the straight grain, whether you 'fussy-cut' or not.

**5** Place the template back in the hole, and remove the window; note that the shiny side of the freezer paper is against the right side of the fabric. Use the cotton setting on the iron to press the template in position. Cut out the tree shape, adding ⅛in seam allowance all around the edge (**b**); remember to add a little extra allowance on the dotted edges (see p15) to ensure that these edges will be covered by the leaves. Mark round shape (see p15).

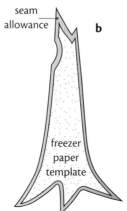

seam allowance

**b**

freezer paper template

**6** Only one template is used for all the leaves, so instead of cutting out lots of individual templates make just one in thin card.

TIP: For an easy way to make an accurate card template, trace the shape onto a small piece of freezer paper but don't cut it out. Iron the freezer paper onto a piece of thin card, then cut out the shape on the traced line. If you cut the shape out leaving a 'window,' this will help with choosing fabric for the shape.

Mark the tip of leaf with T. Some of the leaves (as indicated on the design) use the leaf template in reverse, so mark the back of the card template with R; you will then know which side of the template and window to use for each leaf.

**7** Use the window to help select the best bits of fabric pattern for each leaf. Once you've chosen, drop the card template back in the hole and remove the window. Draw round the leaf template (**c**), using a removable white marker (see p15); when you're drawing round templates, remember to put a piece of fine sandpaper underneath the fabric to stop the fabric slipping. Cut out the shape, adding ⅛in seam allowance all round (**d**).

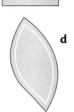

**8** Prepare all the leaves according to your chosen appliqué method for each leaf.

## Appliqué

**9** Using the overlay, position the trunk in place on the background; appliqué the trunk (**e**). Remember to tack the shape in place first if you are needle-turning, and check back to pages 16-19 to refresh your memory of points and curves if necessary. Remember that the edges marked with a dotted line are not turned under as they are covered by leaves. If you're using the fused method, add a little extra on these edges (see p15).

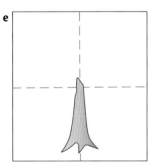
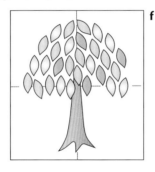

**10** Appliqué all the leaves in position (**f**), using your chosen method. Working on a well-padded surface, press the work from the back.

**11** Now it's time to make the dimensional fallen leaves, these are made using the faced shape technique (p24). On the wrong side of one piece of leaf fabric, mark round the leaf template (**g**). Place this fabric on top of your leaf backing fabric, right sides together; pin in the centre of the leaf, and machine all round on the marked line (**h**), using a straight machine stitch, length 1. Cut out the shape close to the stitching (**i**).

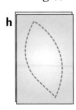

**12** Make a small slit in the centre of the backing fabric – use a pin to separate the layers so that you don't accidentally cut through the top layer too! Turn the leaf to the right side (**j**); roll out the edge of the leaf and finger-press. Stitch these leaves in place (**k**), working ¼in under the edge and stitching only the underneath layer of leaf to the background to maintain dimensional effect. (Or, if you prefer, just use the quilted centre vein to hold the leaf in position.)

## Finishing

### Borders

**13** Trim the background to an accurate 15¼in square with the appliqué centrally positioned.

**14** Follow the instructions on p121-122 (Narrow Border Method) to attach first the inner border (**l**) and then the outer border (**m**).

### Quilting

**15** Follow the instructions on p122 to layer the backing, the wadding and the top fabric. Use two strands of stranded embroidery thread to hand quilt around the trunk and leaves. These stitches are quite bold – about ⅛in long. Quilt the tree trunk first and then the leaves, working from the centre leaves outwards.

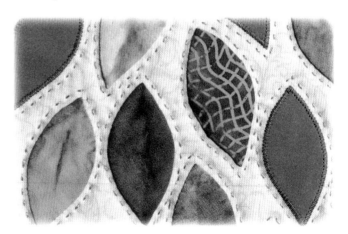

**16** Quilt a few leaves in the background, using regular machine thread and smaller stitches. If you wish, you can use the leaf template as a guide. Quilt a central vein on each of the dimensional leaves.

*Assembling the cushion cover*

**17** You may find that the quilting has made the cushion front a little smaller, so you may need to adjust these measurements slightly. For the cushion back cut one piece of fabric (A) 16½ x 5¼in, and one piece (B) 16½ x 17½in. On piece A make a hem on one long edge by pressing under ¾in twice; machine in place (**n**). On piece B make a hem on the shorter edge by pressing under 1½in twice; stitch in place by machine.

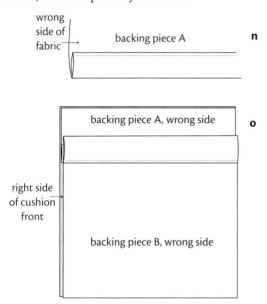

**18** Lay the cushion front right side up on a flat surface, then position the two hemmed rectangles on top, right sides down, so that the hemmed edges overlap and all the raw edges align (**o**). Pin or tack the layers together.

**19** Machine stitch a ¼in seam all around the edge; clip the corners and turn to the right side.

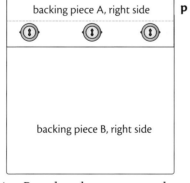

**20** Work three horizontal buttonholes in the hemmed area of section A, spacing the buttonholes evenly. Stitch the buttons onto the hemmed area of section B so that they correspond to the buttonholes (**p**). Alternatively, you could make matching fabric ties to fasten the back opening.

Your project is now complete!

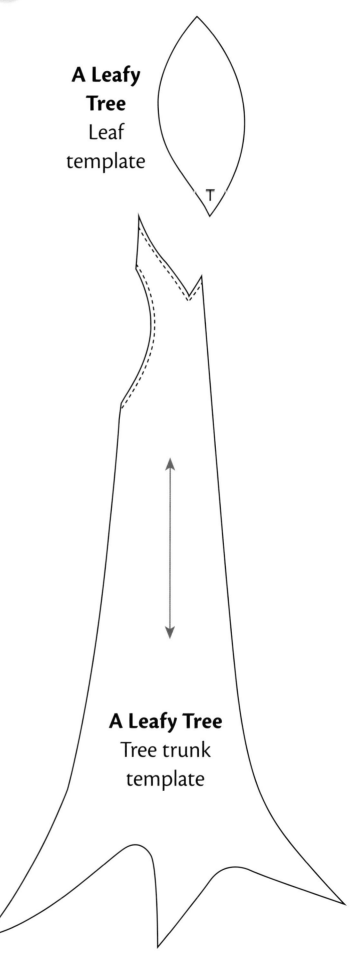

**A Leafy Tree** Leaf template

**A Leafy Tree** Tree trunk template

# A Leafy Tree
full-size design

centre

R

R

R

R

T

T = tip of leaf, all the leaves are appliquéd with the tips pointing towards the ground

*Appliqué techniques*

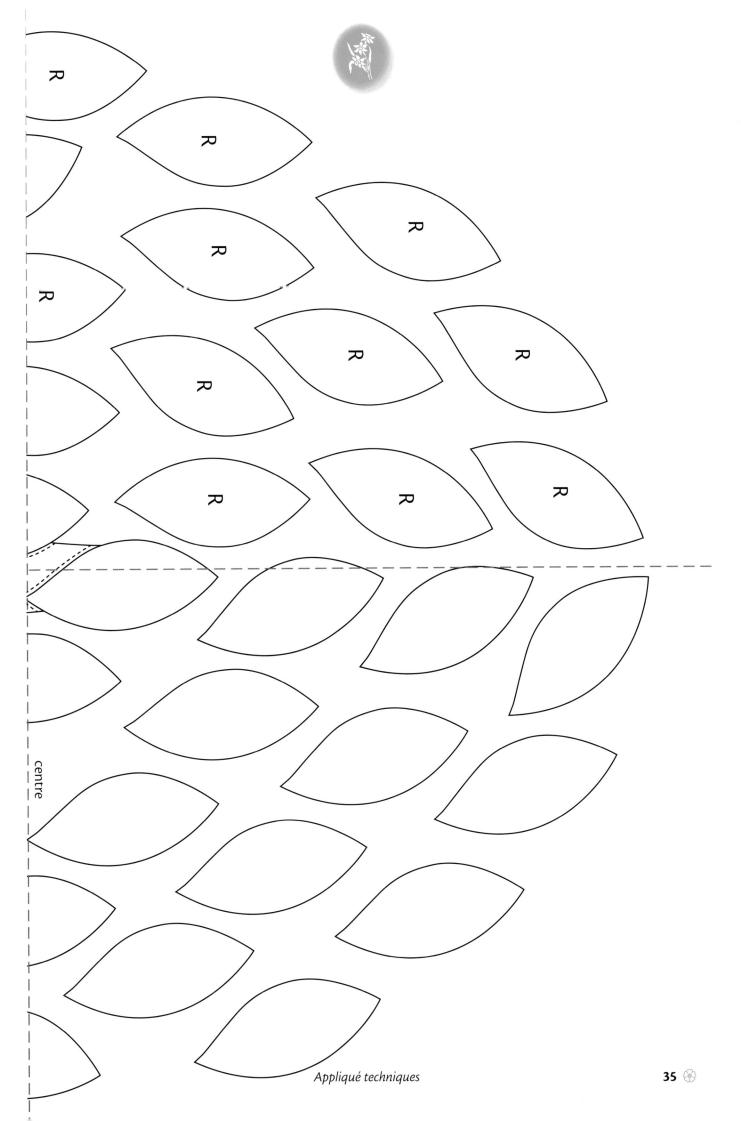

centre

*Appliqué techniques*

# Dimensional flowers

I love dimensional techniques, and usually can't resist adding some dimensional flowers to my designs. I like to experiment with basic shapes such as strips and circles of fabric, using simple techniques of the past such as Suffolk Puffs (yo-yos) and ruching. The results often look more complex than you would imagine, and the flowers are very easy to make. Several of the projects in this book incorporate dimensional flowers; the *Sunflower* panel on p62 includes dimensional sunflowers as well as butterflies and a fence. *Lily Pond* on p45 includes stunning dimensional water-lilies, and *Midnight Dance* on p54 features exotic fantasy blooms. There are also dimensional cyclamens on p70.

To get you started, I've included three basic methods for making dimensional flowers: using fabric circles (working with Suffolk Puffs or yo-yos), ruched fabric strips, and separate gathered petals to make a rose-type flower. As dimensional flowers are usually pleated or gathered in some way, it's best to use the lighter-weight cottons which can be gathered neatly. Silk fabrics make beautiful flowers, but as they tend to fray it's best to practise with cotton for your first attempts!

## Suffolk Puff flowers

Suffolk Puffs are very simple to make, and can be adapted to create several different styles of flower. The resulting blooms may not be botanically correct, but if you use the appropriate fabric, colour and scale, your flower will 'read' as a violet, forget-me-not or buttercup. These little flowers make great 'fillers' in a design; they also look delightful on fabric box-tops, and make very pretty cards.

### Basic method

On the diagrams, I've shown a contrasting-coloured thread so that you can see what's happening clearly, but generally you'll want to match the colour of the thread to the colour of the fabric. You will find a selection of circle templates in different sizes on p127.

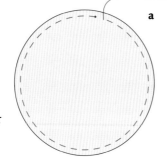

**1** Draw a 1⅓in-diameter circle on fabric and cut it out.

**2** Use regular thread to work small running stitches close to the outer edge on the right side of the fabric (**a**). Fasten on the thread securely, as you'll be pulling the thread up tightly!

**3** Pull up the gathers tightly, and work a double stitch but do not cut the thread. Flatten the shape to make a flat disc with the gathers pulled up in the centre (**b**).

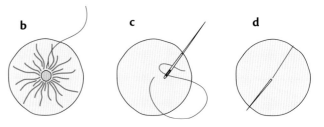

**4** Bring the threaded needle up in the centre of the smooth side, and make a small stitch in the centre. To start dividing the circle into petals, wrap the thread over the edge of the circle and bring the needle back up in the centre. If you catch a thread on the outer edge of the circle (**c**) before passing the needle back up in the centre (**d**), you'll find that the stitch will stay perfectly in position. This is very helpful in achieving evenly-sized petals when you are dividing the Suffolk Puff.

**5** Holding the outer edge between your thumb and first finger, pull up the stitch tightly (**e**). Holding the edge stops it from being pulled either forwards or backwards, and helps you to achieve a nicely-rounded edge on each petal. Of course if you wish you can give a different look to the final flower by deliberately making the edge turn backwards or forwards, to create pointed petals.

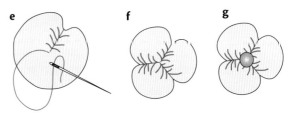

**6** Divide the remainder of the Suffolk Puff in the same way into either three, four or five petals (**f**). Five petals are a bit more challenging to get even-sized, but they look very dainty in small sizes – and when you put several flowers together, any uneven petals aren't noticeable! Work a French knot or add a small bead to the centre of the flower (**g**).

**7** There are many possibilities for making flowers from Suffolk Puffs. You can change the size of the original circle – although over 2in wide it can become a little clumsy. You can change the colour (**h**), and the number of petals (**i**). Depending on the choices you make, your Suffolk Puff flower may become a violet (**j**) or a forget-me-not, and clusters can form a geranium head (**k**) or hydrangea (**l**)! It's a very versatile technique, so have fun experimenting.

## Getting smaller!

If you use a ¾in circle you can make super little flowers, but taking the necessary very small seam allowance can be tricky. Here is a tip from my quilting friend Nancy Kerns. Draw the circle on the fabric (**m**), but work the gathering on the drawn line *before* cutting out the circle. You can then cut very close to the stitching (**n**), and have a very tiny seam allowance with little bulk; this is important when you're working on such a small scale. These tiny flowers can be divided in the same way as the larger ones into three, four or five petals.

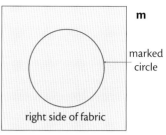

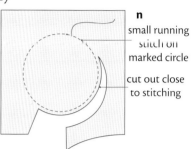

## *Ruched Flowers*

Ruching is another traditional sewing technique which offers many possibilities for dimensional flowers. Depending on the length of the ruched strip you can make a small ruched flower as described below, or a larger one by coiling a longer strip around itself and stitching the rounds together (see the photo of the paeony on p9). I used the small version for the water-lily centre (below), and for the centre of some of the flowers in *Midnight Dance* (p54), where I used narrow ribbon for the ruching. Ruched flowers also adorn the small box shown on p39.

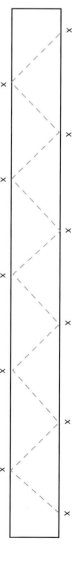

## Small ruched flower

**1** Cut a strip of yellow fabric (or any other colour, according to your preference!) measuring 5½ x 1⅛in. Press a ⅜in turning to the wrong side on one long edge, then press the opposite edge under ¼in. (Note that the turnings will overlap slightly on the back of the strip.) Position the folded strip on the full-size guide diagram (**a**), and lightly mark the X points on each fold.

Using matching sewing thread, work small running stitches as shown on the guide; remember to fasten the thread on securely, as you will be pulling it up tightly.

TIP: At each point marked X make the stitch over the folded edge (b); this helps to create more defined petal shapes when the strip is gathered up.

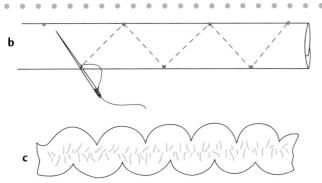

**2**  Pull up the strip until it measures 3in, and work a double stitch; don't cut off the thread. Distribute the gathers evenly along the strip (**c**). You will see that one side of the strip has five petals, and the other has four complete petals and two half-petals – one at each end. This is the side you need to draw up to make the flower. Bring the needle and thread through to point Y – your stitching will have finished on the opposite side of the strip. Work a double stitch and then catch the petal bases, including the two halves as shown (**d**). Pull up the thread tightly and secure it.

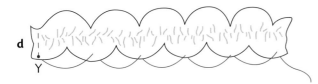

**3**  Bring the thread through to the back of the flower and fold the flower in half, right sides together. Neatly seam the two ends, pulling

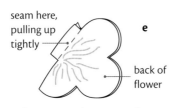

seam here, pulling up tightly

back of flower

tightly between the petals at the outer edge to produce an indentation between the first and last petals (**e**). If the seam is too bulky, trim at this stage.

**4**  The centre can be embellished with beads and/or French knots. A gathered frayed strip (see p53) stitched in the centre is another idea.

## Variations

### Getting smaller

You can make smaller ruched flowers using a narrower strip. Cut a bias strip ¾ x 3½in. (A bias strip has more 'give,' and so works better on the smaller size.) Fold in the raw edges along the length to produce a final strip ⅜in wide; press. Make the flower in the same way as described above, but

use the full-size guide above to work the gathering: with the raw edges uppermost, place the strip on the guide and mark the x points as before. Gather the strip as before, but this time to produce a 2in strip; complete the flower in the usual way.

### Two-colour flowers

You can also create a two-colour version of the ruched flower by joining two different fabrics to create the initial strip. I used this technique for the red and yellow primulas in my *Spring Glade* quilt (see p122).

**1**  Cut one bias strip in red fabric, ¾ x 3½in, and one bias strip in gold the same size. Place the strips right sides together and machine stitch a ¼in seam along the length (**a**); use a short machine stitch, as the seam allowance is small. Trim the seam to ⅛in (**b**) and press it open.

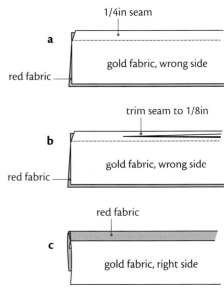

**2**  Press the red strip to the wrong side, leaving ⅛in showing on the right side (**c**). Press under the gold edge to give a finished strip ⅜in wide; trim off any surplus on the back so that the turnings just overlap. Lay the strip on the full-size guide (diagram a under *Getting Smaller*), with the red fabric on the edge that has five complete petals; the finished flower will then have a red outer edge. (You can of course make the flower the other way round, and have a red centre.) Complete the flower as described in *Getting Smaller* above.

## Sewing on dimensional flowers

**1**  Sew on dimensional flowers after any appliqué is stitched and pressed. Pin the flower in position on the right side (**a**).

**3**  Stitch the flower in place with running stitches, working from the back; you will be able to feel the outline of the flower underneath. Stitch just

inside the outer edge of the shape, catching only the back of the flower petals (**b**); this way the flower will maintain its dimensional appearance.

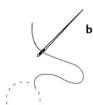

**3** You'll find it best to attach small ruched flowers from the front of the work. Take a stitch through the tip of each petal and into the background; for extra security, also work a stitch in the centre of the flower through to the background

# Roses

These dimensional blooms are easy to make and really versatile. They can make a bold statement in a wall quilt – image a simple rose wreath design with the addition of a few dimensional roses. They also make wonderful fashion accessories, either as a corsage or perhaps to trim a bag or even a hat. They can be glued to a comb or barrette for a hair accessory – think of weddings and other special

occasions, and perhaps use silk, lurex and sheers for a personalised bloom to co-ordinate with an outfit (**a**). I made a be-ribboned rose from a glittery organdie fabric to trim a black evening bag (**b**).

In addition to their fashion possibilities, the roses can be used to adorn fabric-covered boxes. Imagine a memory box, topped with roses made from her wedding dress fabric, as a special gift for a lucky bride! Or how about golden roses for a golden wedding anniversary present? A Christmas gift would be extra special with the addition of a corsage rose pinned to the gift wrap.

*Ruched flowers on a Christmas box, and glittery roses for the festive season to wear or decorate a gift. Note the decorative centres used instead of the bud in the basic rose instructions*

Your roses may be bright, subtle, realistic or abstract – the choice is yours, and as only small pieces of fabric are needed you can enjoy experimenting with your scraps. How about a tartan rose? I suggest that you use a cotton fabric for your first rose; although silks and sheers are lovely, they are a bit more difficult to handle. Each rose will be an individual – it all depends on the fabric you use, and how tightly the petals are gathered or overlapped. However, they will all be beautiful! The project overleaf shows how to make the roses.

**a**

**b**

# Rose Corsages

*Use lightweight cotton fabric for the roses; thicker fabrics won't gather up tightly enough. The rose is made up of three circles of petals and a 'bud' centre. You could make the whole rose from one fabric, in which case ⅛yd would be plenty; or you could choose different tones for each circle, using the lightest for the outer petals, or vary the actual colours – there are several ways to style your rose, as you can see from the examples!*

**Finished size:** *approx 2¾in diameter, excluding leaves*

## What you will need:

- small pieces of lightweight cotton fabric for the petals (see notes on colour above)
- small piece of green fabric for the leaves
- regular sewing thread to match the fabrics
- strong glue (optional)
- 1in brooch back pin
- freezer paper
- thin card for templates

## Preparation

**1** Trace templates A and B onto freezer paper, marking points W and V and the grain line. Trace the leaf and backing circle. Iron the freezer paper onto card, and cut out the templates on the traced outlines (**a**).

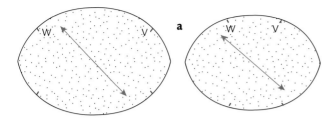

a

**2** When you are cutting the fabric shapes for the petals, take note of the grain lines on the templates.

For the outer round of petals, cut five shapes using template A.

For the middle round of petals, cut three shapes using template A.

For the centre round of petals, cut three shapes using template B.

For the centre bud, cut a rectangle of fabric 3 x 2¼in.

## Making the petals

**1** Begin with the five outer petal shapes, and mark points V and W on each of the petals (**b**). Take one petal and fold it in half lengthways, wrong sides together. Starting from point V, work a running stitch through both layers along the cut edges (**c**). Stop at point W.

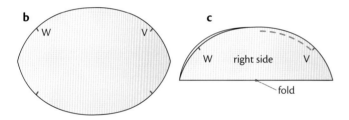

b

W     V

c

W     right side     V

— fold

**2** Fold a second petal in half the same way, and lay it on a flat surface; place the stitched petal on top, matching the raw edges, with the tip of the underneath petal at point W (**d**). Continue the line of running stitch right through both petals (**e**), and stop at point W on second petal. Pull up the thread to gather the petals. Continue in the same way, gathering and attaching the petals until all five petals have been joined together to form a ring; the final petal will overlap the first one.

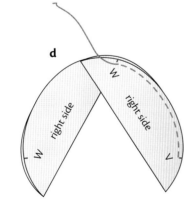

d

W     right side     right side     V

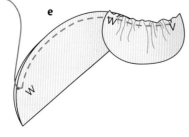

e

W     V

W

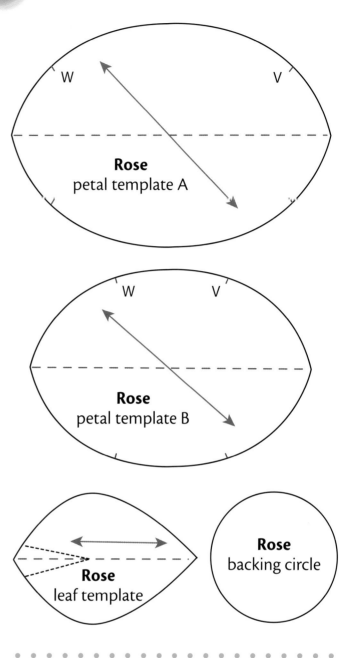

**Rose** petal template A

W     V

**Rose** petal template B

W     V

**Rose** leaf template

**Rose** backing circle

· · · · · · · · · · · · · · · · · · · · · · ·
TIP: The smaller the running stitch, the less the fabric will pull up, so adjust your stitch if necessary to enable you to pull up the petals tightly. You need to be able to pull up the ring of petals to create a centre hole ⅜in in diameter.
· · · · · · · · · · · · · · · · · · · · · · ·

**3** Use the method described above to join the three middle petals, pulling them up tightly.

**4** Use the same method again to join the three centre petals, pulling them up tightly.

**5** Now it's time for the centre bud. On the wrong side of the fabric rectangle, bring down corner X on the longer side to form a triangle (**f**). Fold corner

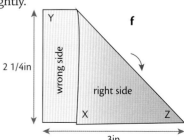

f

Y

2 1/4in     wrong side

right side

X     Z

3in

Y down as shown (**g**), then make a third fold as shown (**h**) to divide the triangle into thirds, turning the last third (point Z) to the back of the bud (**i**).

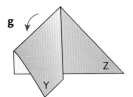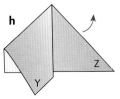

**6** Gather the base of the bud tightly; note that there is a 'tail' left below the bud (**j**). The photo (**k**) shows the three prepared rounds of petals and the centre bud.

## Assembling the rose

**7** Insert the bud through the centre hole of the smallest round of petals, pulling the tail through the centre. Working from the back of the rose, stitch the petals to the bud to secure them; it helps then to splay out the bud a little on the right side, and catch it to the centre petals with a stitch or two to cover any raw edges.

**8** Place the centre in position on the middle round of petals and pull the bud tail through; on the reverse of the rose, overcast the raw edges of these new petals to the centre.

**9** Now place the rose on the outer petals, pull through the tail as before, and on the reverse overcast the outer petals to the middle round of petals.

**10** Check the final appearance of your rose. You may need to catch the back of some petals to the round of petals underneath to 'style' your rose so that the petals fall exactly where you want them – this is not an exact science! Scrunch up the tail from the centre bud and use it to fill out the hollow on the back of the rose, securing it with a few stitches.

## Completing the rose

**11** Use the leaf template to cut three leaves on the straight grain of the fabric (**l**); fold each leaf in half and stitch a small dart as shown (**m**). Glue or stitch the leaves to the back of the rose.

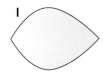

**12** Use the backing circle template to cut a circle of fabric; glue (or stitch) this to the back of the rose to cover any raw edges. Finally, glue or stitch the brooch pin to the centre of the circle.

Glueing is quick, but it looks neater to stitch the fabric circle and brooch pin on the back. Cut a piece of card the same size as the backing circle template, then cut a fabric circle ¼in larger. Follow the instructions on p20 make a fabric circle: press the shape, and remove the card. Stitch the brooch pin securely in the centre of the fabric circle, then stitch the circle to the back of the rose (**n**). Wear with pride!

# *Variation*

## Tucked in tighter

You can make a tighter rose using the same petal templates but assembling the flower slightly differently. For my sample I used a red tonal striped fabric (**a**), which was very effective.

**1** Using the same fabric throughout, cut four petals using template A and four petals using template B.

**2** Start with a smaller petal (one of the shapes cut from template B). Fold the petal in half , wrong sides together, and gather it along the raw edges (**b**), stitching through both layers. Pull the petal up to about half its width before making a double stitch to secure the thread. Don't cut the thread, but take another folded small

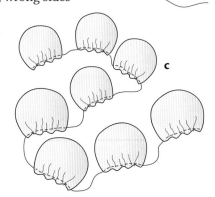

petal and use the same thread to stitch and gather the raw edges as before; start with a double stitch, and leave about 1in of thread between each petal. Continue in this way to string together the four small petals, followed by the four larger ones (**c**): fasten off the thread.

**3** Use the rosebud centre template to cut a circle of fabric, and fold it as shown in the sequence of diagrams (**d**) – note that the circle is not folded completely in half at the start. Gather up the base tightly by wrapping a thread around the shape a few times (**e**) and stitch it to secure.

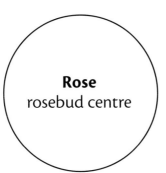

Rose
rosebud centre

d                                              e

**4** To assemble the rose, start by first wrapping one of the petals around the bud; stitch it in place (**f**). Wrap the next small petal around this central shape, overlapping the first petal slightly, and overcast the raw edges on the back of the rose; each petal will overlap the previous one slightly, but you may need to overlap a little more at the start to produce a tighter flower centre (**g**). Continue in this way, adding first the small petals and then the larger ones until all the petals have been attached. Ensure that you keep the back of rose flat while you are stitching the petals in place; stitch only through to the petal immediately underneath, not right through to the centre of the rose (**h**).

f

g

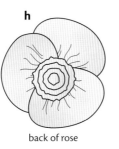
h

back of rose

**5** Finish the back of the rose as for the basic version above.

# Two more leaf styles

## Shaded ribbon leaves

Use a 5in length of wired shaded ribbon about ¾in wide.

**1** Pull up the wire slightly on one long edge to gather the ribbon (**a**). This edge will be the centre of the leaf, so check that the colour will appear where you would like it to be.

a

ribbon wire
pulled up

**2** Fold the ribbon in half. Hand-stitch a seam on the gathered edge (**b**), close to the wire, making a dart at the fold (the top of the leaf) so that the leaf can lie flat at the tip. Stitch the leaf to the back of the rose – you can manipulate the wired edge to produce a lovely dimensional leaf.

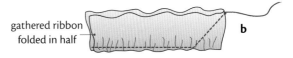

gathered ribbon
folded in half                                    b

## Using printed leaves

You can also cut leaves from a suitable printed fabric; you can make them using the darted method described above (*Basic Rose* step 11), or you could try this fused method. Fusing will produce a firmer leaf, so no dart is used, and the leaf is less likely to fray than if you used the shape without fusing.

**1** Cut out a leaf from the printed fabric, leaving a ½in margin all round (**a**). Cut a piece of fusible web slightly smaller than the cut shape and iron it onto the back of the leaf (**b**).

a           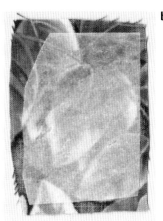 b

c            d

**2** Remove the paper backing and place the leaf on the backing fabric, wrong sides together; iron to fuse the two fabrics together (**c**). Cut out the leaf shape (**d**), and stitch it to the back of your rose.

## Another Easy Flower

This open-faced flower (**a**) is even easier to make! Each petal is made from a circle, folded in half and gathered; choose a lightweight fabric which can be gathered up tightly. You will find the relevant circle templates on p127.

**1**   Use the 2½in template to cut out five circles of fabric, one for each petal.

**2**   Fold one petal in half on the bias (the stretchy direction), wrong sides together (**b**); this will make the petal curl up well. Using running stitches about ⅛in long and ⅛in apart, gather the

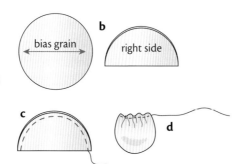

curved raw edges together (**c**). Pull the gathers up tightly and make a double stitch to secure the thread (**d**); do not cut the thread, but move on to the next petal. Gather the next one as before, and continue until all five petals are gathered and joined into a ring (**e**). Fasten off thread. Note that the outer edges of the petals will turn up; adjust the fabric to get a pleasing balanced effect.

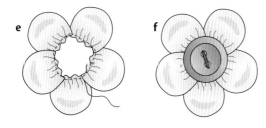

**3**   Cut a 1¼in circle of fabric for the flower base. Stitch the flower to the base, stab-stitching through the base of the petals. Choose a button large enough to cover raw edges of the petals and stitch it in the centre of the flower (**f**), or appliqué a fabric circle (see *Perfect Circles* on p20). There are various ways in which you can embellish the centre with embroidery and beads – just play!

**4**   Trim the base slightly. Finish the back of the flower as given in the instructions for the basic rose.

**5**   This style of flower looks good combined with appliqué and used in a wall-hanging or cushion design. Think of a pretty bedroom cushion strewn with pastel blooms on a softly-patterned background.

**6**   You can combine one ring of outer petals of the basic rose (see p41) with this flower to make a combination flower as shown (**g** and **h**).

Dimensional flowers are fun to make, and can be used in so many different ways. I hope you feel encouraged to use these simple but effective techniques to create your own floral ideas. Over these next pages you'll find four gorgeous projects, each including some more dimensional flower techniques for you to try: fantasy flowers, sunflowers, cyclamen and water-lilies.

## Project 3

# Lily Pond

*Water-lilies are exquisite flowers, and were the inspiration for this narrow wall quilt. I've combined dimensional lilies and leaves with fused appliqué to give an illusion of distance to a peaceful view across the pond. The shaded batik background was a perfect choice to create the effect of the darker foreground receding to the lighter distant reeds and sunny meadows; if you can't find a suitable batik, the background could be pieced. I used the same beautiful batik for the backing and binding to complete the theme. Fused raw-edge applqué was used throughout except for the two faced leaves in the foreground, but of course you can needle-turn the design if you prefer.*

*I stitched the appliqué in place after the quilt was layered, so the appliqué stitching also acts as quilting – two steps in one! I suggest you complete the quilt and binding before you add the dimensional flowers, though; it will be easier without the bulky lilies in place.*

**Finished size:** *approx 26¾ x 13¾in*

## What you will need:

❀ ½yd background fabric (if, as I did, you prefer to have the straight grain running lengthways because of the design printed on the fabric, you will need ⅞yd, and this will be enough fabric for the backing and binding too)

❀ appliqué fabrics:

• small pieces of light green for reeds, mid to darker greens for lily leaves and buds, dark red for the back of the faced leaves. I used a satin-backed dupion fabric for three of the leaves, but you could use cotton fabrics for all the leaves.

• ⅛yd each of three tones of pink, ranging from very light to medium pink, for the lilies

• a small piece of yellow for the lily centres

• small piece of brown for the frog

❀ silk thread or alternative fine thread to match the appliqué fabrics

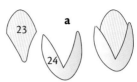

- machine stitching thread to match the dimensional water-lily fabrics
- small yellow beads for the lily centres, black bead for the frog's eye
- freezer paper for templates
- fusible web
- small extra piece of thin cotton wadding for padding the frog
- for quilting:
  - 30 x 16in low-loft wadding
  - 30 x 16in backing fabric (see note above about background fabric)
  - matching thread for quilting. I used fine threads to blend with the background colour at the top of the quilt, but changed to a variegated machine quilting thread about two thirds down to give a bolder stitch
- ⅛yd fabric for binding (see note above about background fabric)

## Preparation

Note that all the separate templates for the fused appliqué and dimensional faced leaves are given in reverse, ready for you to trace onto the paper side of your fusible web.

**1**  Cut a piece of the background fabric to measure 27½ x 14in; mark the centre vertical line with tacking.

**2**  The easiest way to position the appliqué shapes is by eye, using the placement guide opposite to show you how the pieces relate to each other; the arrangement is quite simple, and if you wish you can change it to suit your own ideas. If you prefer, though, you can enlarge the placement guide to full size (enlarge by 224% on a photocopier), then use a light-box to position the appliqué. Go over the lines with a fine black marker to ensure you can see them through the background fabric when it's on the light-box.

### Flat leaves and reeds

**3**  Prepare the seven flat lily leaves and the reeds (templates #1-17) for fused appliqué (see p23). It's a little trickier to fussy-cut with this technique as you are working on the back of the fabric; if you would like to use specific shaded parts of the fabrics on your shapes, follow the method on p22.

### Buds

**4**  Prepare the calyx (#24) and buds (#23) in the usual way using fusible web. For the buds (23) I wanted to make use of the fabric shading, so I used the fussy-cutting method (p22) when I was positioning the fusible web shape on the back of the fabric. Note that a little extra has been added to the bud template as shown by the dotted line.

TIP: Some fusible webs (eg Steam-a-Seam™) have a tacky surface that allows you to fix pieces in position temporarily; if you're using one of these products, you can pre-assemble the buds if you wish. Remove the paper from the prepared calyx and place it in position on the bud, overlapping the shapes slightly (a). Finger-press the two shapes together for a temporary hold – do not iron at this stage or it will stick to the ironing surface! Position the pre-assembled buds on the background and then fuse them in place.

If your product does not enable you to pre-assemble the buds, you will find it easier to fuse each bud (23) to the background and then fuse its calyx (24) on top. Prepare five buds this way.

### Water-lilies

**5**  Pre-assemble two fused water-lily flowers. Prepare the base using template #18, removing the centre of the fusible web shape (see p22). I fussy-cut the fabric to take advantage of fabric shading, so I used a freezer paper window as described on p22.

**6**  Prepare the rest of the flower petal shapes using templates #19-22. Note that a little extra has been added on 19, 20 and 21 as shown by the dotted line; this allows for a slight overlap rather than butting edges together. Remove the paper backing from shapes 19-22 only. Place 19 in position on 18 first, and fuse in place (**b**). Then, in number order, fuse 20-22 in position, overlapping the shapes as indicated by the dotted lines (**c** and **d**). Finally, remove paper backing from 18; your flowers are now ready for fusing in place at stage 9.

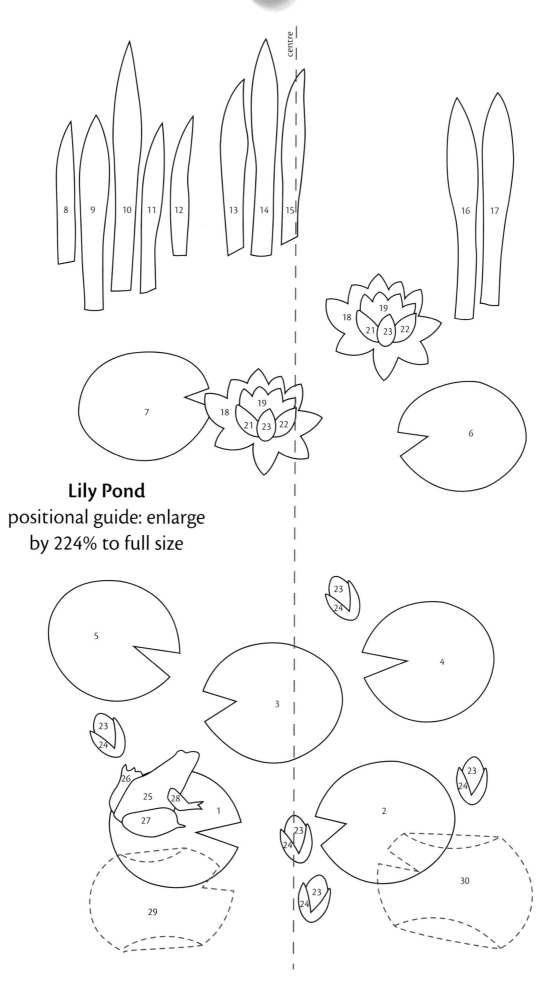

**Lily Pond**
positional guide: enlarge
by 224% to full size

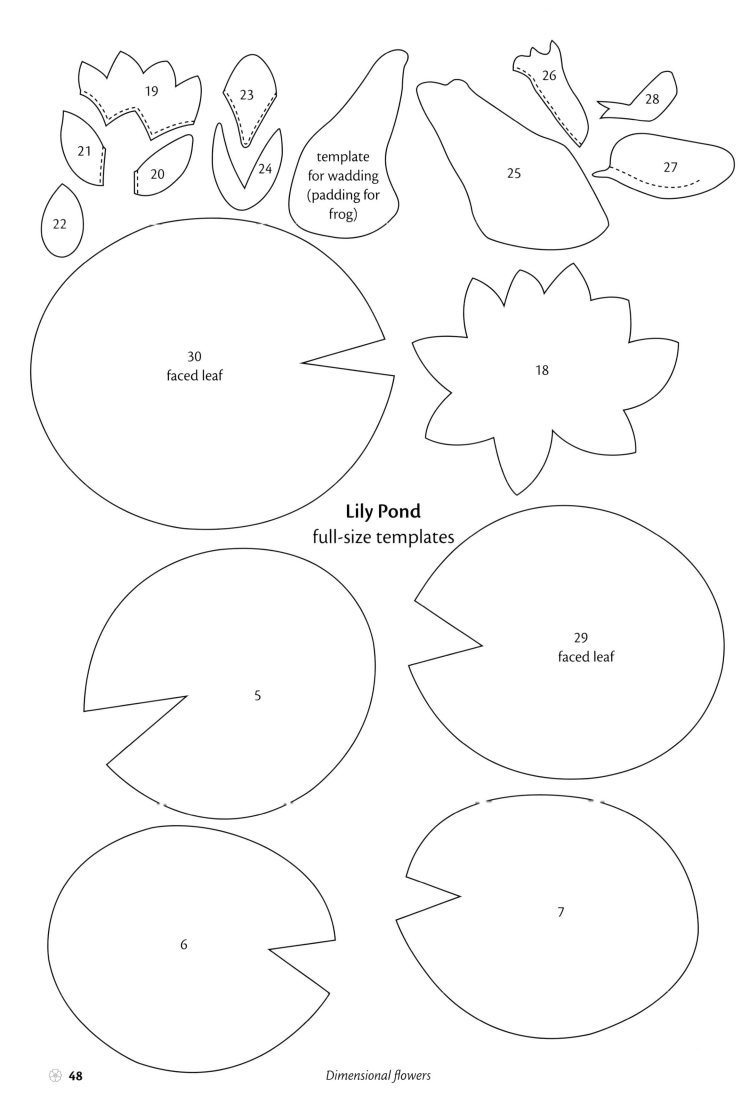

19

23

21

20

24

22

template for wadding (padding for frog)

25

26

28

27

30
faced leaf

18

**Lily Pond**
full-size templates

5

29
faced leaf

6

7

*Dimensional flowers*

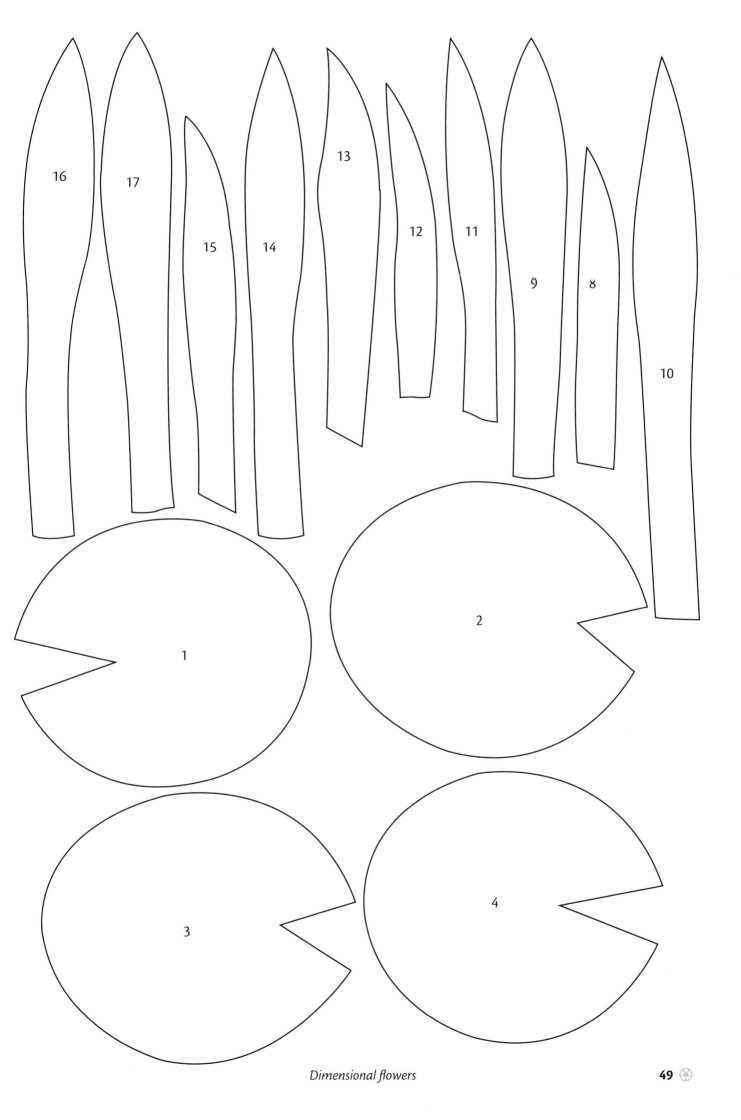

*Dimensional flowers*

## Fusing the shapes in position

**9** Press the background fabric to remove any creases. If you are using a light-box to position the appliqué on the background, tape the design in position on the light-box and place the fabric on top, matching the centre lines; leaf 1 should be about 3¼in from the lower edge of the fabric. Tape the fabric in place.

**10** You'll find it easiest to work in sections, fusing a section at a time, starting at the bottom of the design with leaf 1. Fuse the lily leaves in place, then the buds (**h**). Fuse the lilies in place, then arrange the reeds and fuse them in place near the top of the design (**i**).

**7** Prepare the frog shapes using templates #25-28. Note that a little extra has been added to 26, as shown by the dotted line. Pre-assemble the frog, overlapping the shapes as indicated by the dotted lines (**e-f**); again, you may need to assemble the frog directly on to the background depending on the fusible web you are using.

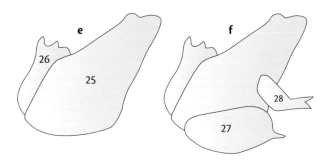

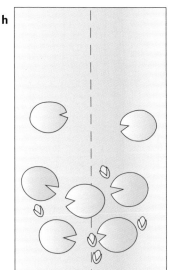

### Faced leaves

**8** Make two faced leaves (**g**), using templates #29 and 30 and following the technique on p24. Note that the templates are reversed, and your finished leaf will have green on top and red underneath; I used a dark red fabric for the underside of the leaf, which shows when the edges of the leaves are folded back. Cut a hole in the centre of the back of the leaf for turning; this is easier than leaving a gap in the seam, and gives the leaf a smoother outer edge.

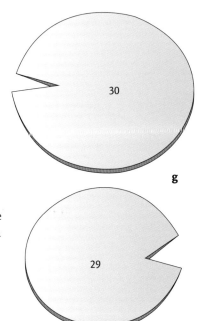

**11** The frog is lightly padded. Use the template on p48 to cut a shape from thin cotton wadding; it's slightly smaller than the frog, so that the edge of the frog can still be fused in place to the background around the wadding. Place the wadding shape on the background and the frog on top (**j**), use the tip of the iron to fuse the edges without flattening the frog. A little mini-iron is helpful for these tricky areas.

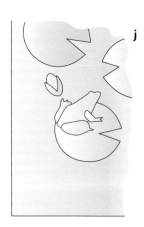

## Appliqué and quilting

**12** Layer the quilt with the wadding and backing, and tack/baste the quilt sandwich to hold the layers firmly together (see p122).

**13** Use a walking foot if your machine does not have dual feed. Also use a knee-lift if possible; it makes raising and lowering the presser foot so much easier when there are lots of stops and starts.

TIP: I suggest that you always do a test piece to check the stitch before actually quilting the appliqué. Make up a little sample sandwich with backing, wadding and top fabric, and adjust the stitch length and width to get the effect you like. Use your intended thread as that can make a difference too. I used fine threads – YLI silk or a #50 cotton for all the appliqué, as I didn't want the stitching to be too dominant.

**14** Working from the centre outwards (to keep the whole piece smooth), stitch the background quilted 'water' lines and incorporate the appliqué as you go along; that is, don't stitch all the appliqué first and then fill in with the background quilted water effect. If the basting threads are likely to get caught in the machine stitching, clip them and move them out of the way as you work the quilting and appliqué.

**15** Start with reed 15 and work across to reed 8, and use the reed templates to quilt some extra reed outlines. Add some quilted 'water' lines in between, and then stitch reeds 16 and 17.

**16** Move on to the two flat water lilies and leaves (6 and 7). Appliqué the reeds, water-lilies and buds with a straight stitch, length 2 – you may need to use a slightly shorter stitch to negotiate the small petals on

**k**

the lilies and buds (**k**). The dotted lines on the diagram (**l**) show interior stitching lines on the water-lilies; quilt these as you work, to define the petals. Appliqué the lily leaves with a zigzag stitch, width 1.5 and length 0.5

(see the TIP in step 12). Quilt the vein markings with a straight stitch.

**17** Appliqué the frog using a narrow, slightly open zigzag, width 1. Appliqué the shapes in number order, noting that 26 goes

**l**

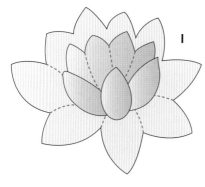

under 25. Either quilt or use a fine liner to mark the detail on piece 27. Add a bead or embroider the frog's eye.

## Adding the dimensional leaves

**18** Machine-stitch the vein lines on the dimensional leaves. Working on the underside of the shapes, catch-stitch the leaves in place onto the background, just making enough stitches to hold the leaves in position. Turn part of the outer edges of the leaves to the front, to show the red undersides, and catch the folded sections in place.

## Finishing

**19** Lay the quilt on a cutting mat and trim it to an accurate rectangle. The appliqué and quilting will have shrunk the work slightly, so it will need to be re-sized; mine worked out at 26¾ x 13¾in, but you can adjust these measurements if necessary. Follow the instructions on p124 to bind the quilt.

**20** Follow the instructions on p52-53 to make one large, one medium and one small dimensional water-lily. Pin the dimensional lilies in place. Slip-stitch the turned edge of each lily base to the quilt, stitching through to the back of the quilt to ensure that it is well anchored. Some of the outer petals on the largest lily will need a few stitches on the back, to attach them to the quilt and prevent the lily from falling forwards when the quilt is hung.

# Making a dimensional water-lily

**1** Using the templates on p127, trace a 5in, 4in, 3in and 2in circle onto freezer paper. Iron these shapes onto thin card and cut them out.

**2** The large lily is made up of four rounds of petals, starting with the lightest tone for the largest outer petals and working through to the deepest tone for the smallest petals in the centre.

Use the 5in circle template to cut four circles from the lightest-tone pink fabric

Use the 4in circle to cut four circles in the next tone, and the 3in circle to cut four circles from the same fabric

Use the 2in circle to cut four circles in the deepest tone.

**3** Cut all the 5in fabric circles in half on the straight grain (**a**). Fold one half-circle in half again, right sides facing and with the straight edges together (**b**), and pin. Repeat with six of the other half-circles (there will be one spare); machine stitch a ⅛in seam and trim the corner (**c**). It will be quicker if you chain-piece the petals. Turn each petal to the right side.

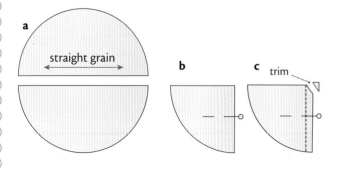

**4** Fold each petal so that the seam lies centrally at the back (**d**). At this stage the raw edges won't match exactly because of the shape of the fabric (**e**); line up the raw edges together – this pulls up the petal and produces a nice upward curl. Pin the raw edges together, and work a running stitch to stitch the raw edges together (**f**). Pull the gathers up tightly (**g**), and work a double stitch to secure the thread; do not cut the thread, but take up the next petal and gather base in the same way. Repeat with all seven petals, and finally join the last petal to the first to form a ring (**h**).

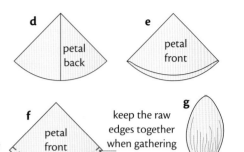
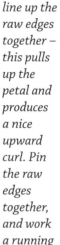

**5** Use the same method to make seven petals using the 4in fabric circles, seven petals using the 3in circles, and seven using the 2in circles. (Note that there will be one half-circle spare in each size.) Join each batch to make petal circles as described in step 4.

**6** It's easier to assemble the lily if the petals are stitched to a base. Cut a 4in square from the outer petal fabric. To assemble the largest lily, mark a 1¾in diameter circle in the centre of this square, on the wrong side of the fabric. Place the ring of outer petals on the right side and pin it in place (**i**); pin with the pins pointing outwards, matching the line of gathered stitching to the circle drawn on the back. Stab-stitch through the base of the petals along the row of gathering stitches, stitching through to the drawn circle on the back.

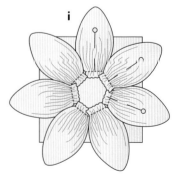

j

TIP: You may find it easier to create the larger lilies by assembling them on a larger piece of fabric stretched in a small embroidery hoop (j).

**7** Place the next-size ring of petals in the centre of the first ring, and stitch these in place through to the base (**k**). Continue in this way until all four rings of petals are sewn in position (**l**).

k                                l

**8** The centre is made as a small ruched flower. For each lily centre, cut a strip of yellow fabric 5½ x 1⅛in; follow the instructions on p37 to create these flowers. To embellish the centre of each flower, add some fringing and a few beads. To make the fringing: from yellow fabric, cut a strip on the straight grain 2 x ½in; choose a fabric which is easy to fray. Work a running stitch close to one long edge, and fray the opposite edge (**m**). Pull up the strip tightly, and fasten with

m

a double stitch; sew the frayed strip to the centre of the ruched flower. Stitch each lily flower centre in position, stitching firmly through to the base, then add a few small beads (**n**).

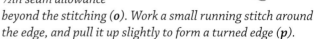

n

**9** To finish the back of the lily, trim the base leaving ½in seam allowance beyond the stitching (**o**). Work a small running stitch around the edge, and pull it up slightly to form a turned edge (**p**).

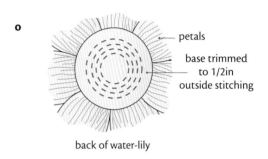

o

— petals

base trimmed to 1/2in outside stitching

back of water-lily

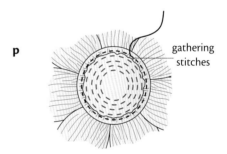

p

gathering stitches

**10** The same method is used to make the medium-sized and small-sized lilies. The medium size has one round of petals made using 4in circles, one round using 3in circles, and one round using 2in circles of fabric. The smallest lily has one round of petals made using 3in circles, and one round of petals using 2in circles of fabric. The medium lily is assembled on a base marked with a 1½in circle; the small lily doesn't really need a marked circle on the base to maintain its circular shape.

## Project 4

# *Midnight Dance*

*At midnight these fantasy flowers come out to dance! For the flowers and the appliqué I used colourful batiks, which really glow on the darker background. This is quite a simple design, suitable for beginners. The appliqué in my original was needle-turned, and I've given instructions for this technique below, but you could equally well stitch the design by machine. Two different types of flowers in varying sizes fill the dancing vase, and I've finished the flowers with a variety of centres; these are fantasy flowers, so feel free to adapt the suggestions to make your own versions. A wavy border complements the dancing theme, decorated with bold big-stitch quilting.*

**Finished size: *21½ x 17¾in***

*Dimensional flowers*

## What you will need:

- ½yd background fabric
- ⅝yd for borders and binding
- for the appliqué:
  - 9in square for the stems
  - small pieces of fabric for the leaves
  - 7 x 6in piece for the vase
- for the flowers:
  - small pieces of lightweight cotton fabrics (as a guide, the largest flower requires five 4in circles)
  - 15in length of organza ribbon, ⅝in wide, for the large flower centres
  - beads for embellishing the flower centres
- silk thread or alternative fine thread to match the appliqué fabrics
- machine stitching thread to match the dimensional flower fabrics
- freezer paper for templates
- for quilting the design:
  - 24 x 20in low-loft wadding
  - 24 x 20in backing fabric
  - thread to match the background fabric for outline-quilting the appliqué
  - coton à broder or similar embroidery thread for the bold quilting (I used variegated thread in the appliqué colours for quilting the border)

## Preparation

**1** Cut the background fabric 21¾ x 18in. Mark the centre lines with tacking; this will help you with the appliqué placement.

**2** Make a tracing of the complete design (p60-61). If you are using a pale background fabric, you may well be able to see the design through it; if necessary, though, use a light-box so that you can see the design clearly. If you're using a very dark fabric, and can't see the design even using a light-box, follow the instructions in the step 3 for making an overlay. Using pencil, or a removable white marker, lightly trace the position of the stems. Remember that you only need to mark the stems with a single line, but extend the lines ¼in under the vase and under the flower positions shown by the circles. Use a small dot to mark the tip and base of each leaf, marking just inside the leaf outline so that the dots will be covered.

**3** If you're working on a very dark fabric, make an overlay (see p12) instead and use this to position the appliqué; just a paper tracing, taped at the top to the background, will be adequate for this simple design. Don't forget to match the centre lines when you're attaching the overlay. Alternatively you could simply estimate the placement of the leaves and vase by eye, using the centre

lines on the background and the full-size design for guidance. There are only a few simple shapes, so feel free to arrange them as you like for your own midnight dance!

**4** Trace the leaves (templates #1-6) and vase (#7) onto the matt side of the freezer paper to make the templates (**a**). Number and cut out the shapes, leaving pattern 'windows' (see p15); use these windows to select the fabric shading, and iron the templates onto the right side of the appropriate fabrics. Cut the shapes out (**b**), adding seam allowances (see p15).

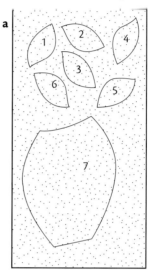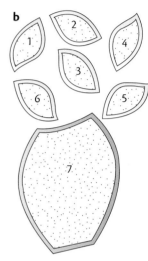

## Appliqué

**5** Use the overlay or marked dots to position all the leaves except leaf 6; this will be added after the vase has been appliquéd. Tack/baste the leaves in place, and follow the needle-turning instructions on p16-19 to appliqué them (**c**).

**6** Cut 1in-wide bias strips of your chosen fabrics for the stems. Use the bias bar method and a ⅛in bar (see p10) to make the stems.

**7** Pin the stems on the marked lines on background, positioning each stem so that it is centred over the line. (If you are using an overlay for positioning, slide each stem under the tracing and line it up with the design on the overlay.)

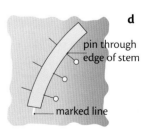

Ensure that the bottom of each stem extends ¼in under the vase, and that the top extends ¼in under the flower, as marked on the design. Appliqué each side of the stems (**d**), stitching the outer curved edge first and easing in the inner edge to produce smooth, flat curves (**e**).

**8** Appliqué the vase in position; where the edge of the vase will be covered by leaf 6, leave this as a raw edge. Finally, appliqué leaf 6 to complete all the appliqué (**f**).

## Finishing

**9** Working on a well-padded surface, press the appliqué from the back. Check that the background is still an accurate rectangle; trim if necessary.

**10** The borders are appliquéd in place by needle-turning the inner edges to the background. Use a photocopier to enlarge the border templates opposite by 200%. Trace templates

A and B onto freezer paper, marking the centre lines and the straight grain; cut out the templates. Template A is used for both side borders and template B for both top and bottom borders. To make it easier to cut out the shaped borders, begin by cutting four strips of fabric border fabric 4 x 19in.

**11** Start with right-hand border. Working on the straight grain, iron template A onto the right side of one border strip (**g**), lining the straight edge up with the edge of the fabric. Cut the shape out, adding a small seam allowance on the curved edge only (**h**). Mark the curved edge of the template on the fabric.

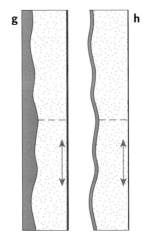

**12** Place the border on the quilt, matching the border centre with background centre line and with the outer raw edges together. Pin in place, pinning in the seam allowance on the inner edge, and remove the template (**i**). Secure the inner edge with a line of running stitch ½in from the edge. Using the same template, repeat the process to make the left hand border and pin it in place. Needle-turn the inner edges of the borders to the background (**j**). On the back of the work, cut away the surplus background fabric behind the borders, leaving a ½in seam allowance.

**13** Using template B, and working the same way as for the side borders, cut out the top border, adding ¼in seam allowance on the curved edge only. Position and tack this border at the top of the design as before, then do the same with the bottom border; note that the top and bottom borders extend over the side borders. Needle-turn the inner edges to the background, continuing across the side borders too (**k**). Trim any excess length off the borders, then on the back of the work cut away the surplus background fabric behind the borders leaving a ½in seam allowance. Remove the centre tacking lines.

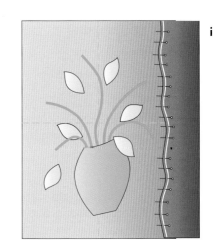

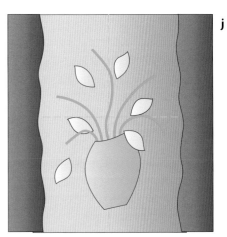

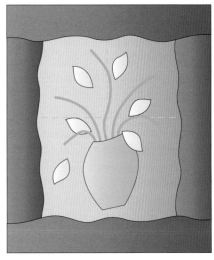

## Quilting

**14** Layer the quilt with the wadding and backing (see p122); tack/baste to hold the layers firmly together. Use a walking foot if your machine does not have dual feed; also, use a knee-lift if possible – it makes raising and lowering the presser foot so much easier when you're outline-quilting the appliqué. Use a thread colour to match background and machine stitch around the vase, stems and leaves, stitching a scant ⅛in from each appliqué shape. (Alternatively you could outline the appliqué shapes with hand quilting.) Machine quilt ⅛in inside the border around the background.

**15** Arrange the freezer paper leaf templates on the background and pin them in place (see the main photograph for suggested placement of the leaves). Mark around the leaf shapes, remove the templates, and hand quilt using a green coton à broder thread for a bold effect. With a regular thread, hand quilt vein lines on the appliquéd leaves and add some contour lines on the vase.

**16** On the border, work bold quilting stitches in coton à broder ¼in from the curved edges. I used stitches ¼in long and ⅛in apart, and marked some guidance dots on the border to help me keep the stitches even. I also changed the thread colour as I went round, using a variegated yellow and a variegated pink and turquoise to echo the colours of the flowers.

## Finishing

### Binding

**17** Trim the quilt to an accurate rectangle and work a running stitch around the edges to hold the layers together. Follow the instructions on p124 to bind the quilt.

**18** Place all the flowers on the quilt as in the photo, but adjust the placement if necessary until you are happy with the arrangement. Pin in place.

### Adding flowers 8, 9 and 10

**19** Sew each flower base to the quilt, tucking under the ¼in seam allowance as you stitch down the edge. When you are adding the dimensional flowers, try to stitch through to the wadding at least to attach the flower firmly on the background – you could also take a couple of stitches through the flower centre. On flowers 8 and 9, catch the underside of the petals to the background about 1in from the centre to keep the petals in place on the background. Note that flower 10 has the petals pushed back, with the petal points against the background. Flowers 8 and 9 have the petals pushed forwards, giving a more dimensional effect. You can choose how you would like to style your fantasy flowers!

### Adding flowers 11 and 12

**20** If you have pre-assembled these on a base, stitch the base to the quilt, tucking under the ¼in seam allowance as you stitch the edge down Work a few stitches in the centre of each flower to anchor it securely to quilt. Alternatively, stitch the flower directly to the quilt as you assemble it.

### Flower 13

**21** This small flower is sewn directly to the quilt without a base.

You now have a beautiful bunch of exotic flowers in your vase!

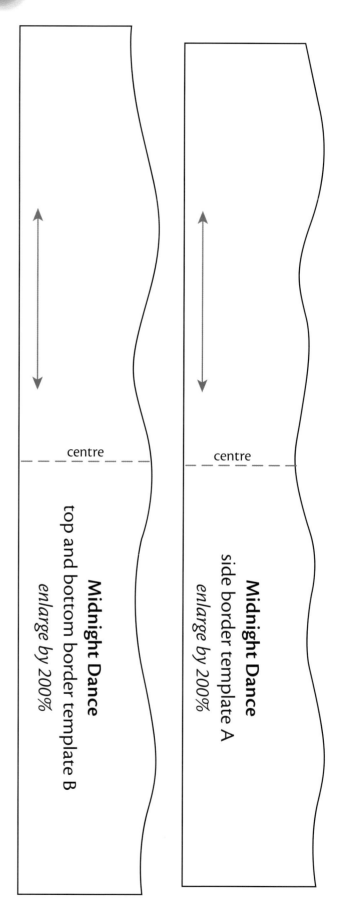

centre

centre

**Midnight Dance**
top and bottom border template B
*enlarge by 200%*

**Midnight Dance**
side border template A
*enlarge by 200%*

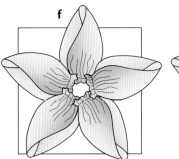

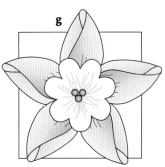

# Dimensional flowers

The flowers are stitched in position after the quilt is layered and quilted. It is then much easier to do the quilting. Also you can attach the flowers more securely through the quilt as well as make a final decision about the placement to give a balanced arrangement. You will find templates for all the circles required on p127.

### Flowers 8 and 9

**1** Using the 4in circle template, cut five circles of lightweight fabric. Fold one circle almost in half (*a*) – note that the raw edges are not level – then virtually into thirds as shown (*b* and *c*).

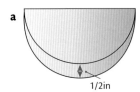

**2** Work a running stitch along the base of the petal, bringing the raw edges together (this will give a curve to the petal). Pull the thread up tightly (*d*) and fasten it off. Make four more petals in the same way.

**3** To make centre, take a 7½in length of organza ribbon and use matching thread to ruche the ribbon. Instructions for ruching are on p37; use the guide to work the running stitch, but in this

seam here, pulling up tightly

back of flower

instance you will have seven petals, and the ribbon is slightly wider than the guide. As it is a very fine ribbon and there are no turned edges, the strip will pull up easily. Catch together the base of each petal and pull it up tightly to form a circle; work a double stitch, seam the ends together, and trim (*e*). (If you don't have any suitable ribbon you could use a bias cut strip of sheer fabric, ⅝in wide, leaving the edges raw.)

**4** The flower is assembled on a base. Cut a small piece of fabric about 4in square and mark a ¾in circle in the centre. Arrange the petals around the circle, with the raw edges on the drawn line; sew them in place by stab-stitching through the gathering at the base of the petals (*f*). Stitch the ruched flower in the centre, catching it through the gathering

stitches to ensure that the raw edges of the petals are covered. Embellish with beads (*g*). Remove the flower from the base by cutting ¼in outside the stitching on the back.

### Flower 10

This is made in the same way as flowers 8 and 9, but the petals are created from 3in circles, and are sewn in position with the smooth side on top and the folded edges underneath. The centre is a small ruched flower, with a cluster of small beads stitched in the centre.

**1** To make the centre, cut a 5½ x 1⅛in strip of fabric and follow the instructions on p37. Make a base as before for assembling the flower; mark a placement circle on the base, and attach the petals with the folded edges on the back of the flower (*a*). Stitch the ruched flower in the centre, catching down the outer edge of its petals to cover the raw edges of the larger petals.

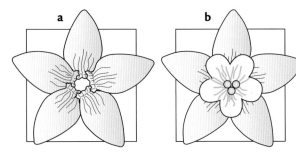

**2** Add a few beads to the centre (*b*), and remove from the base as before. (Note that on this version I have tipped the petals back instead of forward to produce a different effect.)

Flowers 11, 12 and 13 have similar petals to the water-lilies in the Lily Pond project (p45).

### Flower 11

**1** Cut four 2½in circles in your chosen fabric for the outer petals. Follow the instructions on p52 to make seven petals joined in a ring (there will be one half-circle spare).

**2** Use the same method to make seven petals from four 2in circles, and join the petals to make a ring.

**3** Make a ruched flower centre using a 5½ x 1⅛in strip of fabric, folded and gathered as before.

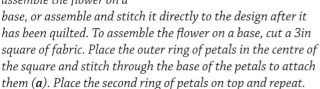

**4** You can either assemble the flower on a base, or assemble and stitch it directly to the design after it has been quilted. To assemble the flower on a base, cut a 3in square of fabric. Place the outer ring of petals in the centre of the square and stitch through the base of the petals to attach them (*a*). Place the second ring of petals on top and repeat.

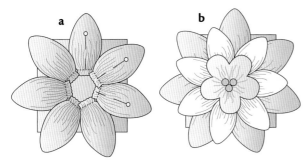

Finally, stitch the ruched flower in the centre and secure it with a few stitches; add a few beads and/or French knots (*b*). Remove the flower from the base by cutting ¼in outside the stitching on the back.

### Flower 12

**1** Cut four 2½in circles of fabric, and follow the instructions on p52 to make a ring of seven petals.

**2** Follow the instructions on p20 to make a ¾in circle for the flower centre.

**3** Choose a loosely-woven fabric (so that it will fray easily), and cut a strip 4½ x ¾in on the straight grain; follow the instructions on p53 to fringe and gather the strip and stitch it into a circle.

**4** Assemble the flower on a base as before. First stitch down the ring of petals (*a*), then add the fringing (*b*), and finally appliqué the circle in the centre. If you would like a raised effect in the centre,

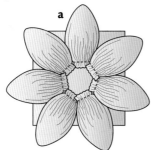

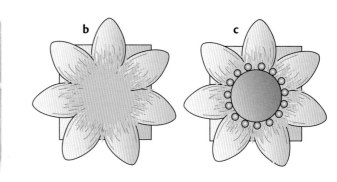

cut a little circle of wadding and position it under the circle before you appliqué it. Finally, embellish the centre by stitching small beads around the centre (*c*).

**5** Remove the flower from the base by cutting ¼in outside the stitching on the back.

### Flower 13

**1** Cut four 2in circles of fabric, and follow the instructions on p52 to make a ring of seven petals.

**2** Make a ruched flower centre using a 5½ x 1⅛in strip of fabric, folded and gathered as before. Stitch the ruched flower

to the centre of the ring of petals (*a*), and embellish the centre with a few beads and French knots (*b*).

This flower does not need a base, as it is quite simple and can easily be stitched directly in position on the design after you've completed the quilting.

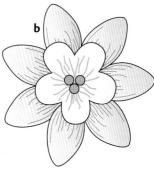

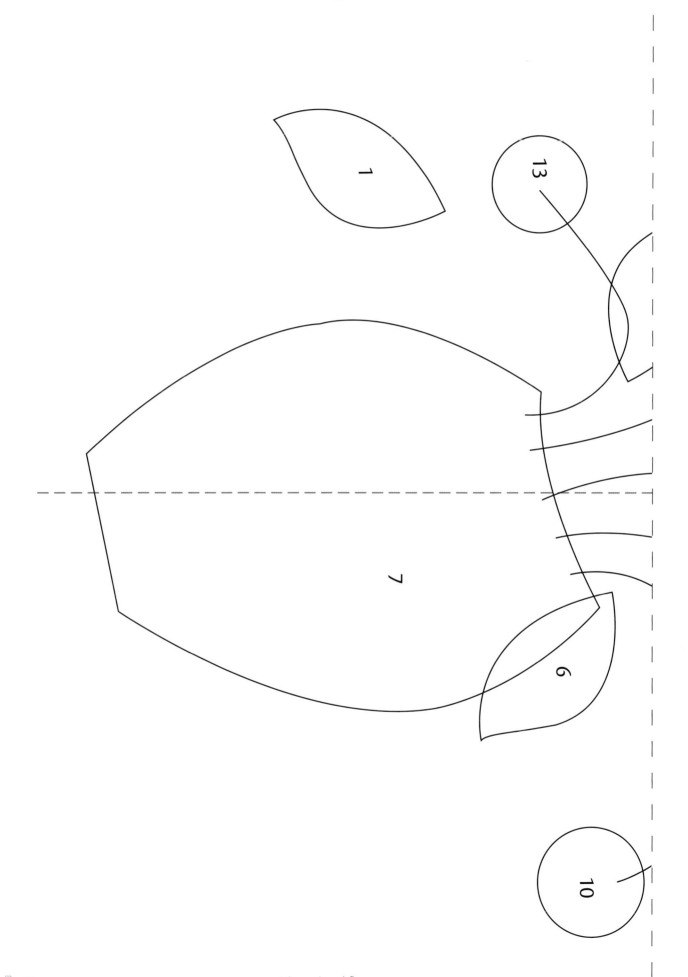

*Dimensional flowers*

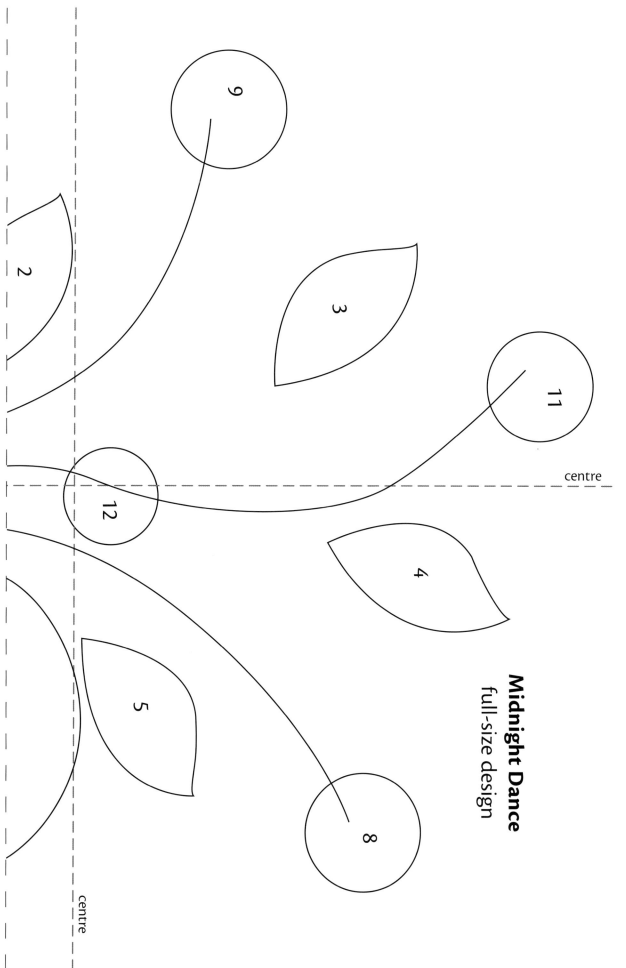

**Midnight Dance**
full-size design

centre

centre

*Dimensional flowers*

# Project 5

# Sunflowers and Butterflies

*Bright yellow sunflowers against a blue sky are one of the joys of summer. Set in a hilly landscape, these sunflowers tower loftily over a rickety fence amidst fluttering butterflies. The design is mainly machine stitched, apart from the dimensional sunflowers. The simple shapes of the appliquéd leaves and stems make this an easy appliqué project to stitch by machine or hand. Instead of piecing the background, you could use one piece of landscape or shaded fabric for a quick and easy wall quilt.*

**Finished size: *24 x 19½in***

*Dimensional flowers*

## What you will need:

- ❁ fabrics for the pieced background:
  mid blue and light blue, 15 x 8in of each
  light green and mid green, 12 x 9in of each
  mid brown and mid/dark brown, 5 x 15in of each

- ❁ for the applique:
  - ♦ small pieces of green for the leaves and stems
  - ♦ small pieces of brown for the sunflower centres
  - ♦ 12 x 18in for the fence posts
  - ♦ 15 x 4in for the fence rails
  - ♦ lightweight fabric for the sunflowers, three strips 2½ x 16in
  - ♦ small piece of shaded orange and a piece of purple for the butterflies – batiks work best

- ❁ for the borders and binding
  - ♦ ⅛yd for the inner border
  - ♦ ⅝yd for the outer border (cut on the lengthways grain)
  - ♦ ¼yd for binding

- ❁ fine thread (eg #50 cotton, YLI #100 silk) to match the appliqué and butterflies

- ❁ machine stitching thread to match the sunflower fabrics, fence posts and background fabrics

- ❁ freezer paper for templates

- ❁ fusible web

- ❁ for quilting the design:
  - ♦ 26 in x 22in piece of low-loft wadding
  - ♦ 26 in x 22in piece of backing fabric
  - ♦ hand and machine quilting thread to match the background fabrics

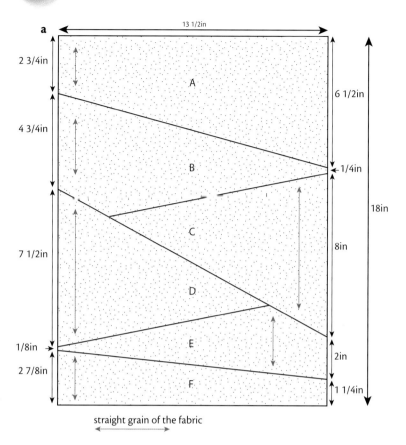

straight grain of the fabric

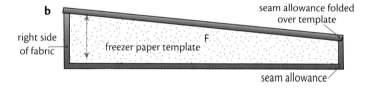

seam allowance folded over template

right side of fabric

freezer paper template

F

seam allowance

## Creating the background

**1** The background is pieced, as shown in the diagram (**a**). On the freezer paper, draw a rectangle measuring 13½ x 18in; mark the measurements given along the sides, then join the marks to create the complete pattern. Label the templates A–F and mark the straight grain lines as shown by the arrows, then cut out the templates.

**2** Lay the templates onto the right side of the background fabrics (refer back to diagram a to check which template goes on which fabric). Iron the templates in position on the straight grain of the relevant fabric, then cut out the shapes, adding ¼in seam allowance all around. Fold the seam allowances over the freezer paper and finger-press firmly (**b**); these creases will become your guidelines for seaming the pieces.

**3** Remove the templates before stitching. As you stitch, check that the seam lines match at the intersections and at the side edges; after completing each seam, press the seam allowances to one side facing towards the lower edge

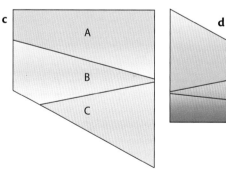

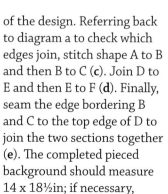

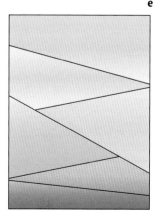

of the design. Referring back to diagram a to check which edges join, stitch shape A to B and then B to C (**c**). Join D to E and then E to F (**d**). Finally, seam the edge bordering B and C to the top edge of D to join the two sections together (**e**). The completed pieced background should measure 14 x 18½in; if necessary, square it up accurately.

## Stems and leaves

**4** To prepare the leaves, trace templates #1-6 onto the paper side of fusible web (note that the templates have been reversed for this technique). Cut out the shapes, adding ¼in extra all round, and remove the centre of each shape. Iron the fusible web shapes to the back of your chosen leaf fabric; cut out the leaves on the traced lines, and remove the paper backing (**f**). (See the instructions for fused appliqué on p22.)

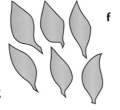

**Sunflowers and butterflies**
leaf templates, full-size

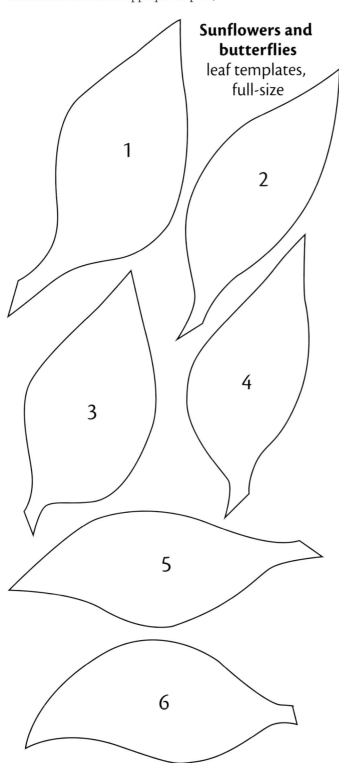

**5** For the stems, cut ¾in-wide bias strips in the following lengths:

stem X 8½in     stem Y 7in     stem Z 9in

To prepare the stems, follow the instructions for *Stems, Method 1* on p27. Press the stems and arrange them on the background as shown on the positioning guide (**g**).

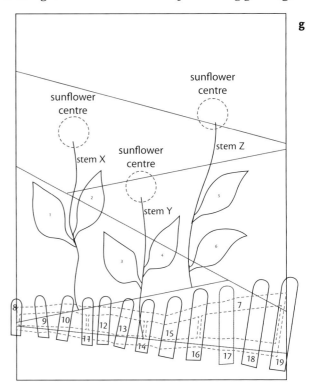

Where stems X and Z meet the D/E seam, undo the seam a little and insert the stems into the gap; re-stitch the gap. Do the same where stem Y meets the E/F seam. The tops of the stems will be covered later by the sunflowers. Pin the stems to the background, placing the pins at right angles.

**6** Position the leaves as shown in the positioning guide, tucking the ends of the leaf stalks under the stems. Tack the stems in position, and then fuse the leaves in place (**h**).

**7** Machine down each side of the stems using a small zigzag stitch, length 1 and width 1 (**i**). Appliqué the leaves, using a zigzag stitch length 0.5 and width 1 to cover the raw edge.

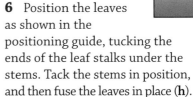

*Dimensional flowers*

# Making the sunflowers

**1** Take one of the 2½in strips of sunflower fabric and cut it into eight pieces, each measuring 2½ x 1¾in, for making the petals. On each petal, place the short sides together and finger-press the centre (**a**); unfold, then on one long edge of each petal press ½in turning to the wrong side (**b**).

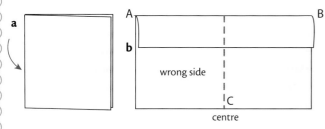

**2** Fold each petal as shown (**c**), with the lower edges together. If points A and B do not meet level in the centre C, adjust the first turning to make it either slightly smaller or slightly larger. You'll find it best to do a trial petal first, to judge the position of the first fold, then fold all the other petals under by the same amount.

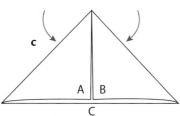

**3** Gather the lower edge of each petal, ⅛in from the edge; pull the thread up very tightly and fasten it off (**d**).

**4** Make the sunflower centre using the circle technique described on p20. You'll find the appropriate circle templates

on p127 – or you can use pre-cut Mylar circles. Cut out a card circle, 1¾in diameter, then cut out a fabric circle 2⅜in diameter; follow the instructions on p20 for making and pressing the circle. Cut a piece of thin wadding slightly smaller than card circle, and slip it inside the centre of the gathered fabric circle (**e**).

**5** Press the background on the reverse at this stage before stitching on the sunflowers. Mark the position of the sunflower centres, as shown on the placement guide, with a 1½in circle. Arrange the petals around the marked circle on the background, with the base of each petal extending over the pencil line by a generous ⅛in. To help you arrange the petals evenly, pin four petals at the quarter positions first (**f**) then pin the other four in between. Note the position of the pins.

**6** Place the padded centre in position on the sunflower (**g**), and check that the raw edges of the petals will be covered. If necessary, move the petals slightly further in rather than stretching the centre to fit, as this will distort the background. Remove the centre so that you can stitch the petals in place.

**7** Use small stab stitches to catch the sunflower petals in place, working just below the gathering stitches to ensure that the stab stitches will be covered later by the padded centre. While they are just pinned in place, the petals will overlap; however, as you stitch the petals in place, push them apart so they just touch at the stitching line. This will make the petals more dimensional than if they are stitched overlapping.

**8** Cut a small piece of wadding and place it in the centre of the ring of sunflower petals to fill the little hollow. Pin the sunflower centre in place and stitch neatly around it, going right through the petals to the background so that you create an indent round the edge of the centre circle. (Because of the thickness of the layers, you'll need to make the stitch in two stages.) Be careful not to pull the stitching too tight as this will distort the background.

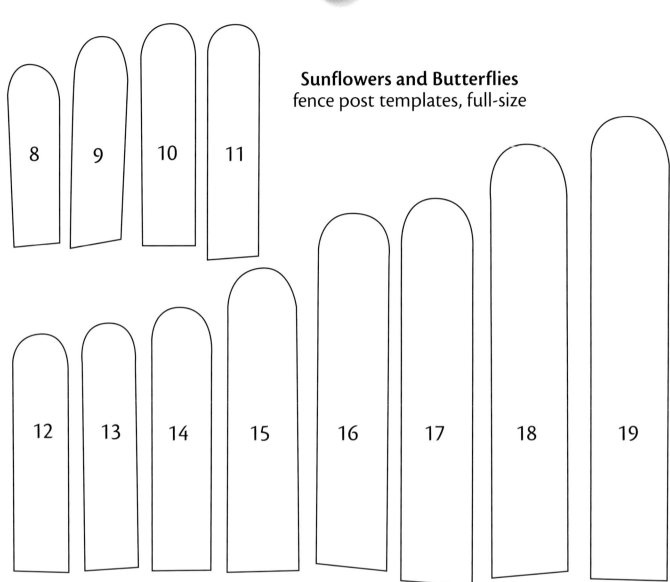

## Sunflowers and Butterflies
fence post templates, full-size

8
9
10
11
12
13
14
15
16
17
18
19

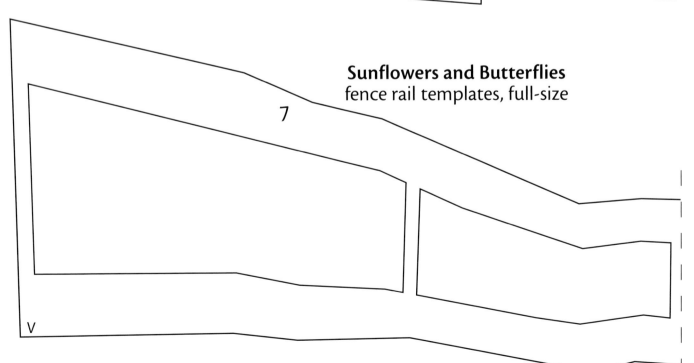

## Sunflowers and Butterflies
fence rail templates, full-size

7

V

## Adding the borders

**8** For the inner border, cut two 18½ x 1¼in strips for the sides and two 15½ x 1¼in strips for the top and bottom (if the dimensions of your background have altered during the appliqué, trim it to an accurate rectangle and adjust the border lengths accordingly). Using ¼in seams, add the side strips to the background and press the seams towards the border. Add the top and bottom border strips in the same way.

**9** For the outer border, cut two 20 x 2½in strips for sides and two 19½ x 2½in strips for the top and bottom. Use the same method as in step 8 to add the outer border (**j**).

## Making the fence

### *Fence rail*

**10** Trace template #7 (fence rails) onto the paper side of the fusible web. (The template has already been reversed.) Note the connecting bars – I've added these to keep the shape stable as you work with it. Cut out the fusible web shape, adding an extra ⅛in on all edges (**k**). Iron the web shape on the back of the fence rail fabric, and cut out the shape on the drawn line (**l**); remember to cut out the spaces between the rails, leaving the connecting bars (**m**).

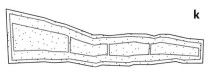

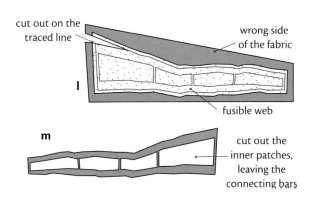

**11** Remove the paper backing. Place the shape on the pieced background so that point V is 1in above the bottom inner border on the right-hand side, and point W is 2½in above the same border on the left-hand side (**n**). The end of the rail will overlap the left border slightly, and sit just inside the right-hand border.

**12** Fuse the rail in position on the background. Use a small zigzag stitch (length 0.5 and width 1) to appliqué the rail in position. There is no need to stitch the connecting bars – they will be covered by the fence posts.

### *Fence posts*

**13** The fence posts are made as faced shapes (see p24). Trace templates #8-19 onto freezer paper and cut them out.

**14** Cut the fence post fabric in half to give you two pieces each measuring 6 x 18in. Iron all the freezer paper templates, shiny sides down, onto the wrong side of one of the fabric pieces; position each template on the

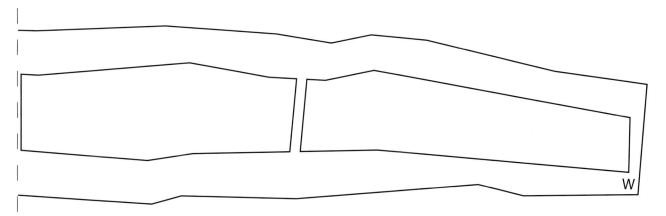

straight grain of the fabric, and leave a ½in gap between the templates to allow for the seam allowances. Put the two pieces of fabric together, right sides facing, and pin in between the templates to keep the layers together. Machine round the templates with a short machine stitch, leaving a gap in each one for turning (**o**).

**15** Cut out each shape, trimming close to the stitching, but leave ¼in at the gap (**p**) – this will make it easier to turn in the edges and close the gap later. Pin each post to its numbered paper template as you cut it out; you need to know which is which so that you can position them correctly on the quilt later. Trim the corners if necessary to reduce the bulk.

**16** Use the straw method (see TIP) to turn the shapes to the right side; turn each end of each fence post separately using the straw. Once each shape is turned, roll out the edges and pull out the corners; press the shapes carefully, and invisibly stitch the gaps closed. Pin each template back onto the finished post for ease of identification!

TIP: This is a great technique for turning small shapes to the right side; it saves a lot of frustration! Take a drinking straw – you only need a short length – and push it up inside the shape to be turned (**q**). Use a small stick with a blunt end to push the end of the

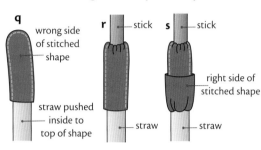

shape a little way down inside the top of the straw (**r**). Keep the stick in position while you slide the rest of the shape up the straw and over the stick (**s**). Remove the stick and straw, and you can easily finish turning the shape – it works like magic! You can purchase commercial turning-stick sets, as used by doll-makers, but the straw method works fine for these shapes.

## Making the butterflies

*The butterflies are made from two layers of fabric bonded together with fusible web. Either use the same fabric for both the top and the backing, or two different fabrics; use a contrast fabric underneath if you want it to show through cut-outs on the wings. I used an orange shaded fabric for the underside of each butterfly, and for the top of the three medium and one small butterfly. A purple top fabric was used for the other small butterfly and the large one.*

**1** *Trace the butterfly templates (#20-22) onto the paper side of the fusible web. (The butterflies are symmetrical, so there's no need to reverse the templates.) Trace one large, three medium and two small butterflies. Cut out the shapes adding ⅛in (**a**). Iron the large and one small fusible web template on to the wrong side of the purple fabric (**b**), and the remaining butterflies onto the orange fabric. Cut out butterflies on the traced lines; cut out the small inner patches from the purple*

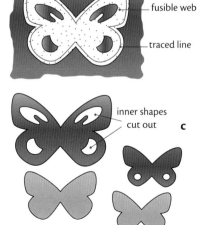

*butterflies, so that the backing fabric will show through the holes. Remove the paper backing from all the shapes (**c**).*

## Finishing the quilt

### Quilting and binding

**17** Layer the quilt top with the wadding and backing; follow the instructions on p122 to tack/baste or safety-pin the layers firmly together. Use a walking foot if your machine does not have dual feed; also use a knee-lifter if possible – it makes raising and lowering the presser foot so much easier when you're outline-quilting the appliqué. Quilt 'in-the-ditch' the pieced background seams, stopping where necessary to avoid stitching over the appliqué shapes.

**18** Use a thread colour to match the background and machine stitch around the stems and leaves, stitching a scant ⅛in from each appliqué shape. Quilt a few cloud shapes in the sky – I did these by hand. Also quilt by hand around the sunflower centres, under the petals, to keep the layers of the quilt secured in this area; this will ensure that the sunflowers sit well on the background. Finally, quilt the inner and outer border seams in the ditch.

**19** Trim the quilt to an accurate rectangle, and work a running stitch around the edge of the quilt to hold the layers together, easing in any fullness to keep quilt flat. Cut 2⅜in wide strips for the binding, and follow the instructions on p124 to bind the quilt, working with a ⅜in seam.

### Completing the appliqué

**20** Place the fence posts in position on the quilt, using the positioning guide and the project photograph for guidance. Remember, though, that your fence doesn't have to be exactly the same as mine – you can arrange your posts to make the fence as rickety as you like! Just ensure that posts 11, 14 and 16 cover the connecting bars of the fence rail. Lightly catch the posts in place with a few stitches just under each post, catching only the underneath fabric layer.

**21** Arrange the butterflies on the quilt. To attach them, use the same thread that was used for stitching the bodies and work a few stitches near the body, stitching right through to the back of the quilt; the wings are left free, which gives them an attractive three-dimensional quality.

## Sunflowers and butterflies
### fence post positioning guide

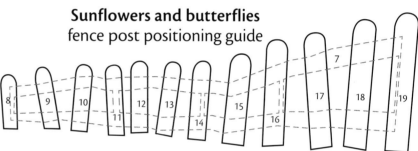

**2** *Place the butterflies on the wrong side of a piece of backing fabric, leaving ½in between the shapes; fuse the butterflies to the backing fabric (d). Use a matching fine thread to work a machine zigzag stitch around the outer edge of each shape. For the body of each butterfly, use a brown fine thread and work several rows of machine stitching side by side to build up a body shape between the wings.*

**3** *Use sharp small scissors to cut out the butterflies close to the machine stitching (e). The butterflies will be attached to the quilt later.*

## Sunflowers and butterflies
### templates, full-size

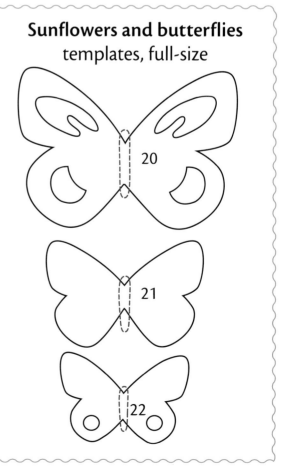

## Project 6

# Cyclamen Pot

*Cyclamens make beautiful houseplants. The upright blooms, with their graceful petals, vary in colour from white through pinks to deep red, and are complemented by attractively-marked leaves. The leaf backs and the stems often have a reddish tinge. For my cyclamen I chose a soft pink for the blooms, and set the terracotta pot in a Victorian jardinière; I used a soft, patterned background and borders to continue the Victorian theme. I have previously made magenta cyclamens for a brighter look, and cream ones for a subtle effect –*
*so choose the colour-scheme that you prefer.*

*The jardinière is constructed from strips made using a very narrow bias bar, and the base is lined. The design is mainly needle-turned appliqué, with the addition of dimensional flowers and leaves. The challenge is finding suitable fabric for the leaves, which can have quite distinctive markings. Use a pattern window (see p15) to help you identify fabric designs which might work. Alternatively, you could use fabric paints or bleach to create visual interest on a plain fabric. For the flowers, soft, lightweight but closely-woven fabrics are the best choice, as the appliqué shape is very narrow at the base of the flower. Also the dimensional flowers need to be gathered tightly, so they too are more difficult to make in thicker cottons.*

*There are many techniques used in this small wall quilt – refer back to the Appliqué Techniques section (p14-19) for reminders and more information if necessary. Remember that although the instructions here refer to needle-turned appliqué, you could machine appliqué the design if you prefer. You could also adapt the design by making a simpler jardinière. On p79 you'll find an alternative version, which you'll find easier to stitch if you are new to appliqué; in this version the appliquéd cyclamen flowers and some of the leaves have simpler shapes, and the jardinière is plainer. Another way to simplify the appliqué is to make all the flowers dimensional and arrange them on the background as you wish; you may need to space them a little differently from my version, then adjust the stem positions to match.*

*Mix and match these suggestions to personalise your design, choosing your preferred methods. This book is all about making choices!*

**Finished size:** *16½ x 13in*

## What you will need:

- 14 x 11in background fabric
- fat quarter for outer border and binding
- for the appliqué:
  - fat quarter for the cyclamens and inner border
  - scraps of green and dark red for the leaves;
  - ⅝in bias strip (12in length in total) for the stems
  - 10in square for the jardinière
  - 6in square for the pot

- silk thread or alternative fine thread to match the appliqué fabrics
- machine stitching thread to match the dimensional flower and leaf fabrics
- freezer paper for templates
- stranded embroidery thread in yellow and dusty pink
- for quilting the design:
  - 18 x 15in low-loft wadding
  - 18 x 15in backing fabric
  - thread to blend with the background fabric

## Preparation

**1**  Mark the centre lines on the background with small tacking stitches (see p12). Use the full-size design on p72 to make an overlay (p13) and attach it in place, then mark the stem positions on the background, marking only the solid lines. (Alternatively, you could just use the overlay to place the stems without marking their exact positions.)

**2**  Prepare freezer paper templates #1-4 for the appliquéd leaves – note that leaves 2 and 4 are partially covered by dimensional faced leaves. The covered edges are shown by dotted lines on the templates, but ensure that you trace off the whole shape of each leaf to create its template. Prepare templates for petals #8-13 – note that separate templates are given for 8, 9 and 10. Prepare templates A and B for the jardinière.

**3**  From the cyclamen fabric cut four 14 x 1in straight strips; reserve these for the inner borders. Cut two pieces 12 x 4in and reserve these for the dimensional cyclamens.

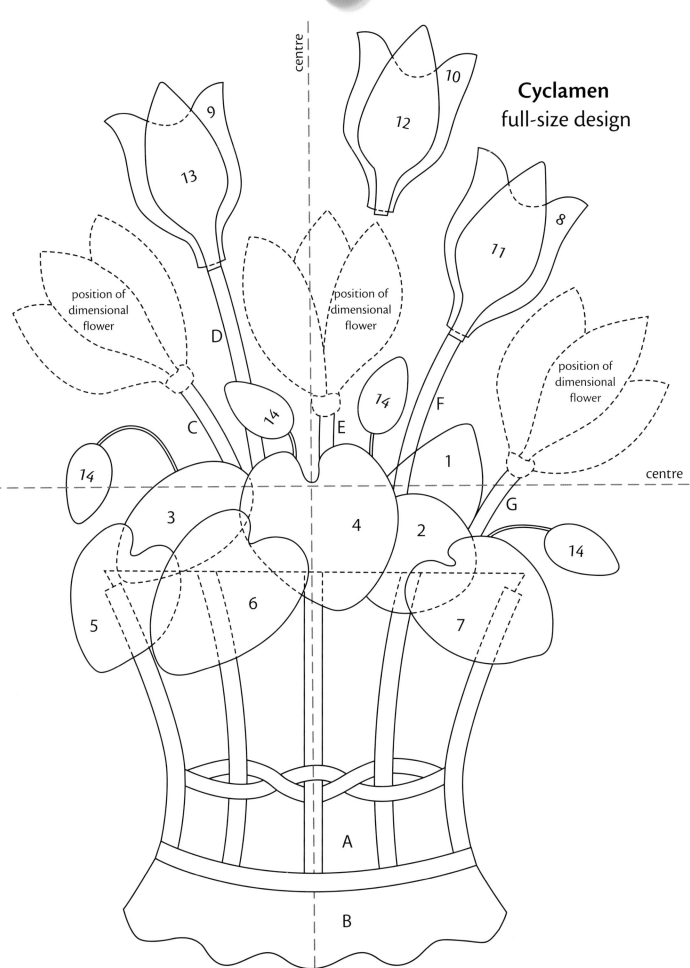

Cyclamen
full-size design

position of
dimensional
flower

position of
dimensional
flower

position of
dimensional
flower

centre

centre

    *Dimensional flowers*

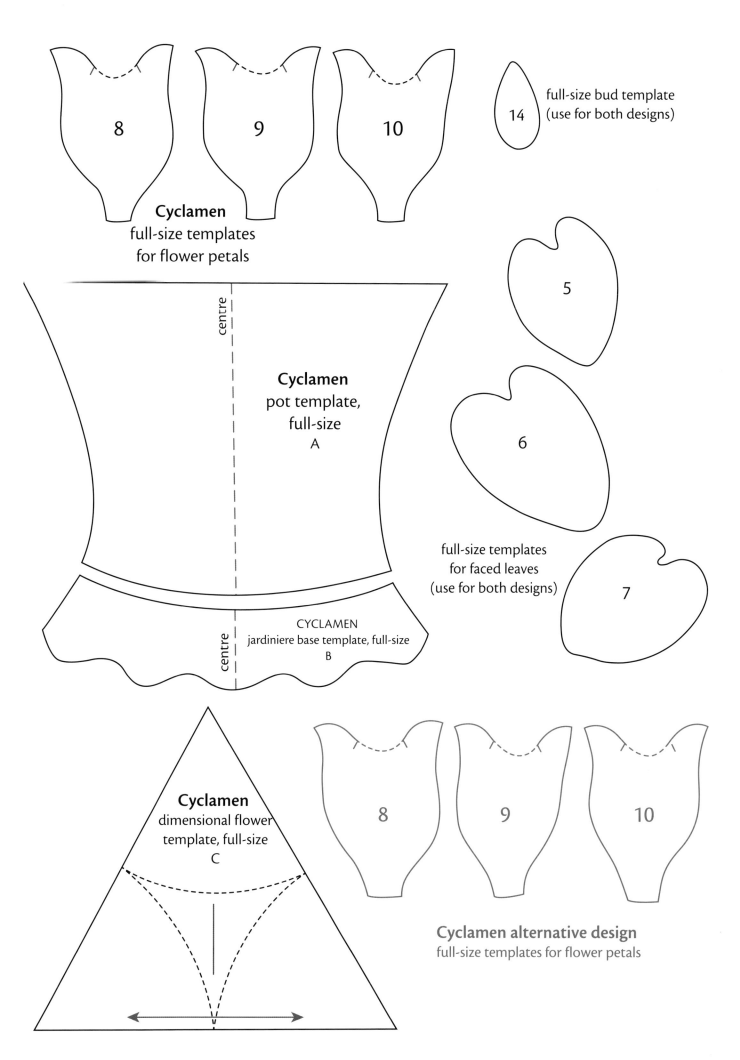

8

9

10

14

**full-size bud template**
(use for both designs)

**Cyclamen**
full-size templates
for flower petals

centre

**Cyclamen**
pot template,
full-size
A

5

6

full-size templates
for faced leaves
(use for both designs)

7

centre

CYCLAMEN
jardiniere base template, full-size
B

**Cyclamen**
dimensional flower
template, full-size
C

8

9

10

**Cyclamen alternative design**
full-size templates for flower petals

# Appliqué

## Making the jardinière

**4**  Iron template A onto the right side of the pot fabric; cut this shape out without adding a seam allowance. Use the overlay to position the pot on background; it should match the top dotted line of the jardinière, and fit just inside the outer side edges. Attach the pot with running stitches round the outside edge.

**5**  Cut 1in-wide bias strips of fabric for the ribs of the jardinière and the weaving. Use an ⅛in bias bar to make the finished strips – an electrical tie would be even better as it's made of a thin plastic (see p10). Take a strip for the left-hand outside rib and place it just below the top of the pot as shown (**a**); pin in place. Position the strip so that it just covers the side of the pot, and allow an extra ½in at the lower end before cutting off the surplus, as shown in the diagram. Check with the overlay that the position is correct.

**6**  Take two 4½in lengths of the prepared strips for the weavers. Place the two strips together under the outside rib, using the overlay to position them; leave about ½in extending outside the jardinière, and overlap the strips on the inside edge as shown (**b**). Pin the weaving strips at the overlapping point. Pin (or lightly glue) the outside rib in place, but only as far as the base. Appliqué the inner edge only of the rib as shown on the diagram; note – only stitch up to the start of the base. Trim the excess ends of the weaving strips and appliqué the outside edge of the rib – again only to the start of the base (**c**). (This will enable you to trim the ribs later.)

**7**  Fold the weaving strips back out of the way, and pin the remaining ribs in position as shown on the design; place the centre rib first, then the end one on the right-hand side, and finally the last two, evenly spaced. Allow an extra ½in at the lower end of each rib as before (**d**).

**8**  Thread the weaving strips through the ribs as shown on the design, overlapping them as before where they thread under the last rib. Stitch down the inner edge of the right-hand end rib in the same

way as you did the first rib (**e**). Trim the excess from the weaving strips and stitch down outer edge, again stopping at the start of the base (**f**).

**9**  Appliqué the remaining ribs, catching down the weaving strips and stopping at the base. You may need to add a little extra stitching to the weaving to keep it flat and even.

- - - - - - - - - - - - - - - - - - - - - -

TIP: You might find a little dab of fabric glue helpful for holding the ribs and weaving strips in place before stitching.

- - - - - - - - - - - - - - - - - - - - - -

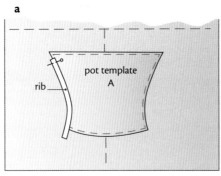

a

pot template A

rib

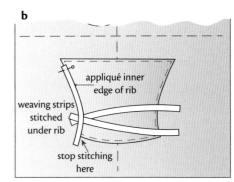

b

appliqué inner edge of rib

weaving strips stitched under rib

stop stitching here

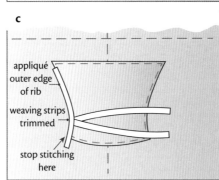

c

appliqué outer edge of rib

weaving strips trimmed

stop stitching here

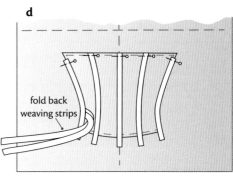

d

fold back weaving strips

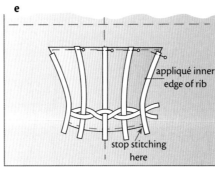

e

appliqué inner edge of rib

stop stitching here

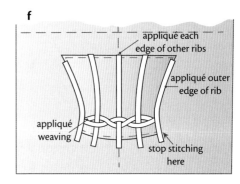

f

appliqué each edge of other ribs

appliqué outer edge of rib

appliqué weaving

stop stitching here

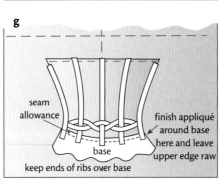

g

seam allowance

finish appliqué around base here and leave upper edge raw

base

keep ends of ribs over base

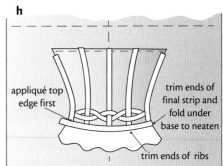

h

appliqué top edge first

trim ends of final strip and fold under base to neaten

trim ends of ribs

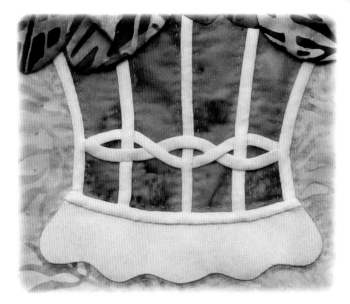

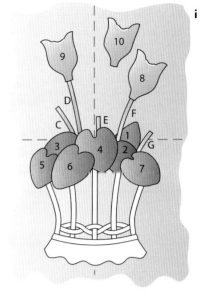

in the background and lighter tones for those in the foreground.

**14** Leaves 5, 6 and 7 are made as dimensional faced leaves (see p24). I used a reddish fabric for the underside – although it doesn't really show! Note that these templates have already been reversed so that they are the correct way round once they've been faced.

**15** Sew on the dimensional leaves; catch down the underside just enough to hold the leaves in position and leaving the edges free.

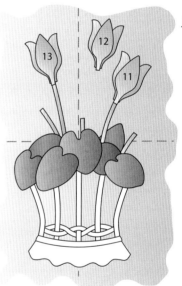

*Flowers*

**16** Appliqué petals 8, 9, and 10 (**i**); remember that any edges marked with a dotted line are not turned under but left as raw edges.

**10** As I used a very light fabric for the jardinière, I lined the base to give me a better depth of colour and to prevent the background and seam allowances from showing through. If this isn't necessary with your chosen fabric, just appliqué the base in the normal way. On p98-99 you will find various ways of lining fabric shapes. For this design I backed a piece of lining fabric with fusible web and cut out the base shape with no added seam allowance. I then fused the lining shape, on the bias, to a piece of the appliqué fabric; position the freezer paper template back on the right side of the base, using a light-box or window if necessary to match the shape up with the lining on the reverse. This method gave me a very crisp outline to the wavy base. Position the base and appliqué it around the sides and lower edge; leave the top edge raw, but held down with a running stitch (**g**).

**11** To complete the base, take a length of the prepared bias strip and place it in position between the ribs and the base, extending ¼in at each end. Appliqué the top edge of the strip first and then trim the ends of the ribs; fold the ends of the strip under the base at the side edges to neaten them (**h**), then finish stitching the strip in place.

*Stems*

**12** Use a ⅝in-wide bias strip and the fine stem method (see p27) to appliqué the stems in position. Keep the stems narrow, especially D and F, as the top end of each one needs to be covered by the narrow part of the flower. Note too that stem F is appliquéd after leaf 1 is stitched down, but before leaf 2 is appliquéd. Remember to extend the stems ⅛in under the leaves and flowers to ensure that the raw edges are covered.

*Leaves*

**13** Follow the instructions on p15 to prepare the appliqué shapes for leaves 1-4, then appliqué them in numerical order. Note that leaves 2-4 are appliquéd all the way around, even though they are partially covered by dimensional leaves. I used darker tones for the leaves

**17** Appliqué petals 11, 12 and 13 (**j**); the registration marks on the underneath shapes will show you where to position these upper petals on each flower. Note that these shapes extend a little at the base of the flower (**k**).

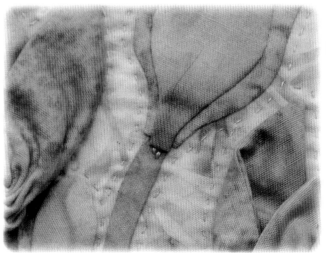

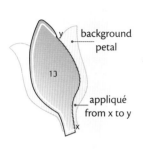

TIP: When stitching a very narrow shape, such as the base of these petals, trim the seam allowance under the first side after you've stitched it as shown. This will reduce the bulk of the seam allowance, and allow the opposite side of the shape to be turned under more easily. (This edge too might need to be trimmed a little more than usual if the shape is very narrow.)

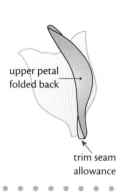

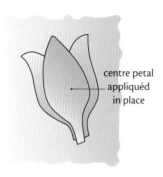

**18** Embroider two small straight stitches as the base of the flower (**see k** on p73).

## Buds

**19** Make a card template for the bud (template #14). These small, rounded shapes will be easier to make with card templates, although you can use a freezer paper template and needle-turn the shapes in the usual way if you prefer.

**20** The card template is used in the same way as a circle template when you're doing the perfect circle technique (see p20), as shown (**l**). Draw round the bud template on the wrong side of the fabric and cut it out, adding a ¼in seam allowance. Work a small running stitch, ⅛in from the edge, leaving the ends free at the start and finish. Place the card template centrally on the wrong side of the shape and pull up the stitching to gather the fabric over the card, twisting the ends together.

**21** Press the shape firmly on the wrong side, loosen the threads and remove the card. Adjust the gathers to regain the original shape, and appliqué the bud in position. Make and appliqué all four buds in the same way, then embroider the bud stems using stem stitch.

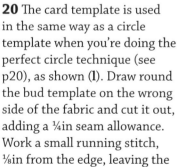

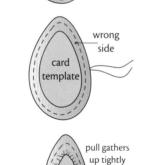

# *Making dimensional cyclamens*

**1** *The cyclamen is made from a double layer of fabric. Trace template C onto freezer paper, marking the straight grain, the position of the slit, and the gathering lines. Cut out the template (**a**).*

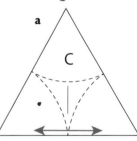

**2** *Take one of the 12 x 4in strips of cyclamen fabric and iron the freezer paper template onto the wrong side. Draw round the template, then remove the template and repeat the process to mark three shapes as shown (**b**), leaving enough space between the shapes to add ¼in seam allowance. Pin this piece of fabric to its matching piece, right sides together; pin in the centre of each shape to keep the layers together.*

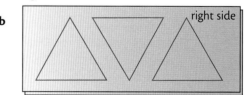

**3** *Machine around each shape on the marked line, using a short machine stitch and starting in the centre of one side (**c**); overlap the stitching for a few stitches at the end.*

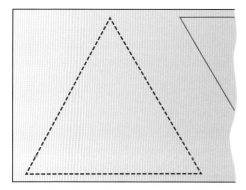

(*Alternatively, use the freezer paper as a guide for your stitching. Iron the template in place and machine round it using a short stitch. Repeat this process twice to make three flowers in total. The same template can be used several times before it loses its 'stick.'*)

**4**  Whichever method you have used, cut the shapes out, adding a scant ⅛in seam allowance; trim the seam allowance at the points as shown (**d**). Lay the template back on one shape and push a pin through at each end of the marked slit to determine where to make the cut; mark the position of the cut between the two pins on the back. Do the same with the other two shapes, then cut each slit along the marked line; separate the layers of fabric with a pin to ensure that you only cut through one layer (**e**).

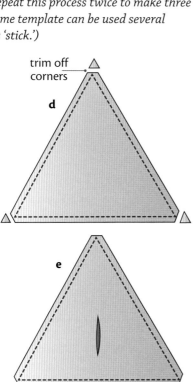

trim off corners

**5**  Turn each shape to the right side; roll out the seam and the points to give a good shape (**f**), and press lightly.

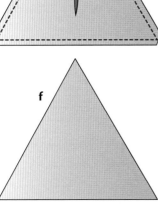

**6**  On each shape, work a line of gathering stitches along the curved dotted line as shown on the template. On the right side, using matching thread, fasten the thread on securely in the centre of one side of the shape and work

small stitches in a curved line across to the opposite side, from 1 to 2 as shown (**g**). Pull up the stitching tightly and work a double stitch to secure the thread before working the next section. Repeat, stitching from 2 to 3 to gather the second section (**h**); after working the last section in the same way, by stitching from 3 to 4, secure the thread but don't cut it. Turn the gathered shape over; the turning slit is now in the centre, and will be hidden inside the flower as you do the next steps (**i**).

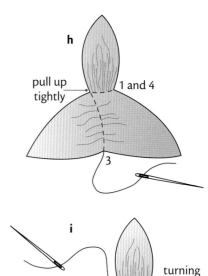

pull up tightly  1 and 4

turning slit

**7**  Fold the flower as shown (**j**), keeping the cut inside the flower base and bringing the two side petals together to make an upright flower. Work a few stitches through the original gathering to nip in the shape more tightly. Catch the outer petals together with a few stitches at the back. Note that the flower can be used either side uppermost (see the photo of the main quilt).

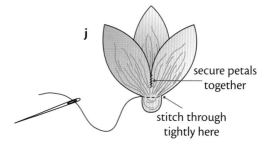

secure petals together

stitch through tightly here

**8**  For a simpler version of the dimensional flower, cut a single layer only of a closely-woven batik fabric and proceed from step 6 above to give a 'raw-edge' flower. This could work well with a machined version of the design.

*Dimensional flowers*  **77**

## Finishing

### Adding the borders

**22** Working on a well-padded surface, press the appliqué from the back. Trim the background to 13½ x 10in (it's easier to do this before adding the dimensional flowers).

**23** Pin the dimensional cyclamens in position on the design, then stitch them in place, working from the back and only catching the backs of the petals (**m**). Your design is now complete.

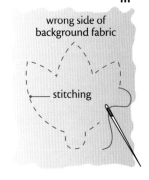

**m**

wrong side of background fabric

— stitching

**24** Add the inner border, using the 1in-wide strips you cut earlier; stitch the side borders on first, trimming them to fit once they're stitched in place, then the top and bottom strips in the same way (see p121).

**25** For the outer borders, cut four 13½ x 2¼in strips; attach the side borders first, and then the top and bottom borders.

### Quilting and binding

**26** Layer the backing, wadding and quilt top, smoothing the layers out flat; tack/baste the layers together (see p122). Outline the appliqué design by hand quilting a very scant ⅛in from the edge of each appliqué shape. Quilt each side of the jardinière ribs, and add a vein line on leaf 4. Also quilt in the ditch the strip at the top of the jardinière base – this defines the shape better.

**27** Quilt the background as desired. I used a scattering of French knots; you could work some diagonal lines instead, or free machine quilt the background. Work a line of quilting just inside the inner border. Finally, work a line of quilting ¼in beyond the inner border.

**28** If you chose the alternative version of the jardinière, you will need to add some additional quilting as it's too big a shape to lie flat. One attractive possibility is to quilt contour lines as shown on the design.

**29** Trim the quilt to an accurate rectangle; work a small running stitch around the edge of the quilt to keep the layers together neatly. Cut 2⅜in-wide strips for the binding, then follow the instructions on p124 to bind the quilt.

## Alternative cyclamen design

**1** *Prepare the background and overlay as in step 1 of the main project, but using the alternative design opposite.*

**2** *To make the jardinière template, trace template A (including the base) onto freezer paper; iron the template onto the fabric, and cut it out adding the seam allowance on all edges except the top edge.*

**3** *Appliqué the fabric shape to the background, leaving a small gap at each side as shown on the design. Leave the top edge raw as it will be covered by the dimensional leaves, but secure it to the background with running stitch.*

**4** *Cut a bias strip of fabric 1in wide and around 5in long, and use an ⅛in bias bar to make a narrow band. Appliqué it in position as shown on the design, tucking the ends under at the gaps in the side edges to neaten the raw ends. (Or, if you prefer, you could use a narrow decorative braid for this strip instead.)*

**5** *Appliqué the stems, leaves and buds as in the first version.*

**6** *The flowers are constructed using unit appliqué. Trace alternative templates #8-13 onto freezer paper; 8, 9 and 10 are given separately, and 11, 12 and 13 should be traced from the design. Mark the registration marks onto templates 8, 9 and 10, and cut all the templates out.*

**7** *Cut a 3in square of cyclamen fabric. Iron template 8 onto the right side and draw round it, adding the registration marks as shown (**a**). Iron template 11 onto a piece of cyclamen fabric (this could be fussy-cut), then cut*

*the shape out and mark round the template in the usual way (**b**). Position 11 on the marked 8 shape, matching the registration marks (**c**); appliqué 11 to 8 as shown (**d**), stopping at the registration marks. Leave the base unturned. Cut out 8, adding the usual seam allowance (**e**). This prepared unit can now be appliquéd in position on the background (**f**); if you wish, you can cut away some of the fabric behind 11 to reduce the bulk. The lower edges of both 8 and 11 are turned under together. Appliqué all three cyclamen flowers in the same way. Complete the design as in the original version.*

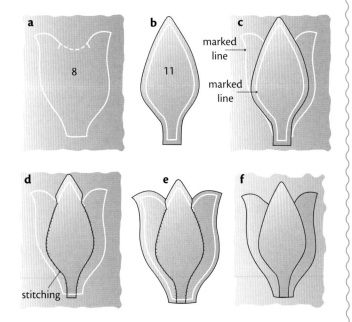

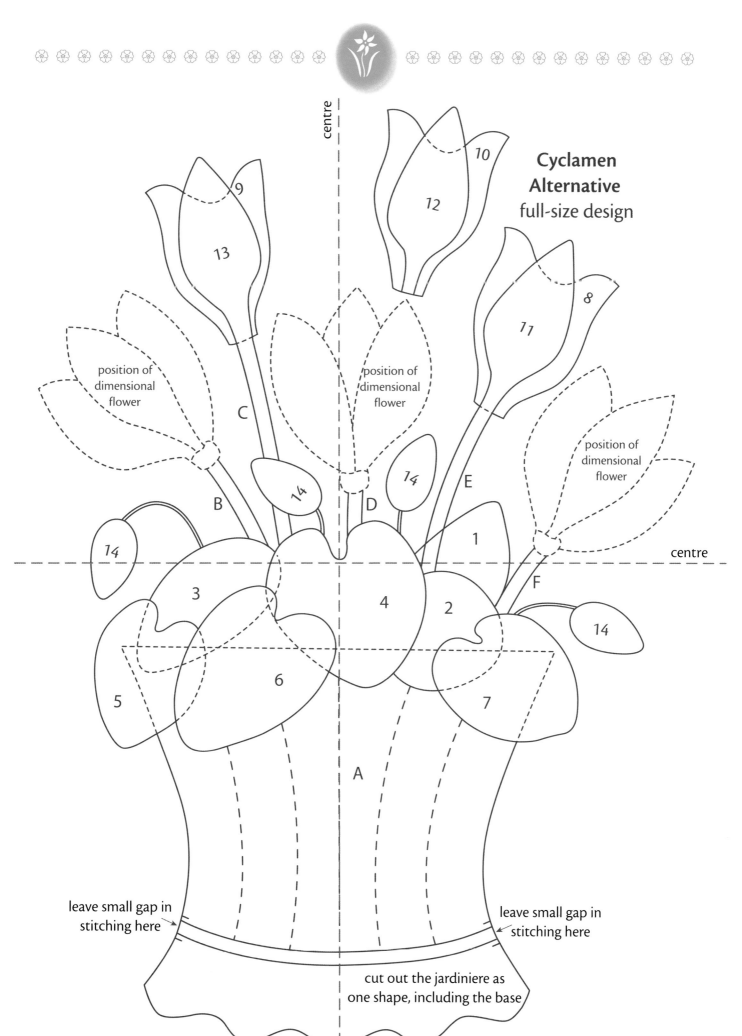

centre

**Cyclamen Alternative** full-size design

9

10

12

13

11

8

position of dimensional flower

position of dimensional flower

position of dimensional flower

C

14

B

D

14

E

14

1

centre

3

4

2

F

14

5

6

7

A

leave small gap in stitching here

leave small gap in stitching here

cut out the jardiniere as one shape, including the base

## Christmas projects

### Project 7

# Robin Wreath

*We all love sewing for Christmas, making special gifts for family and friends as well as decorations for our home. This small wall quilt features a cheerful robin in a traditional wreath of holly and ivy. Although you might not want to display it all year round, it's great for an annual seasonal appearance to brighten up your home. I have designed and stitched two versions – one to stitch by hand, and a smaller, alternative version to stitch by machine (which might be useful if time is short!) In the main quilt the design is hand appliquéd and hand quilted, with an interesting pieced border that sets off the centre block. This border style makes a lovely frame for a one-block design, and would also work well for a cushion. In this project you will be able to practise making perfect circles, points and curves, as well as using the 'unit appliqué' technique to appliqué the robin.*

**Finished size:** *approx 18in square (the appliqué design is 10in square)*

### What you will need:

- ⊛ 14in square of background fabric
- ⊛ ⅜yd for the outer border and the binding
- ⊛ ¼yd for the red border triangles
- ⊛ for the appliqué:
  - ✦ scraps of greens for the leaves (choose a closely-woven fabric for the holly leaves, as there are lots of points and curves)
  - ✦ red/orange for the berries
  - ✦ brown, rust and beige for the robin
  - ✦ brown for the branch
- ⊛ silk thread or alternative fine thread to match the appliqué fabrics
- ⊛ freezer paper for templates
- ⊛ stranded embroidery thread in greyish-brown, dark brown, and two tones of light green
- ⊛ for quilting the design:
  - ✦ 20in square low-loft wadding
  - ✦ 20in square backing fabric
  - ✦ fine thread to blend with the background fabric
  - ✦ regular machine thread to blend with the border fabric
  - ✦ gold thread

- ⊛ clear plastic and fine marker for making the robin overlay

### Preparation

**1** Follow the instructions on p12 to mark the centre lines on the background with small tacking stitches. Make an overlay and attach it (see p12), then prepare the freezer paper templates in the usual way.

**2** Use the freezer paper templates to prepare all the leaf shapes, marking round the templates and cutting the shapes out with seam allowances; fussy-cut the fabric for the ivy leaves to get interesting markings on the leaves.

### Appliqué

**3** Cut a ¾in bias strip for branch; use the fine stem method (see p27) to appliqué a slightly tapered branch. Now appliqué all the leaves in number order.

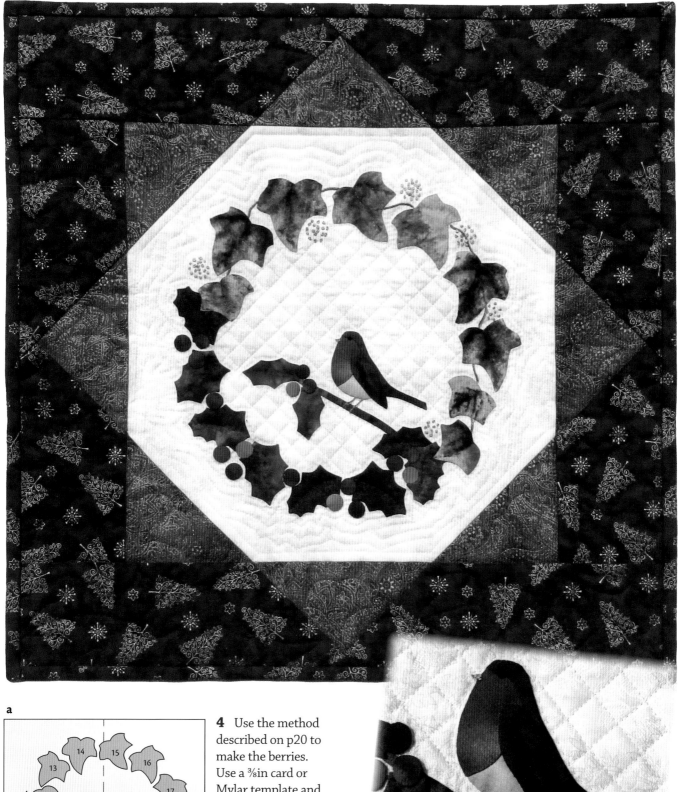

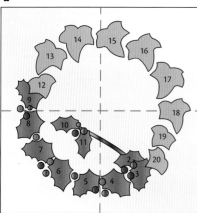

**a**

**4** Use the method described on p20 to make the berries. Use a ⅜in card or Mylar template and cut a ⅞in circle of fabric for each berry; you will find the templates for these circles on p127. Use a few different tones of red and orange fabric for variety.

You could make a few smaller berries using a ¼in template, but these are a little trickier and you can make all the berries the same size if you prefer. Prepare and appliqué the berries in position as shown on the design (**a**).

**5** Follow these instructions for unit appliqué to make and appliqué the robin; as I mention on p13, it's helpful to make a separate clear plastic overlay when assembling birds.

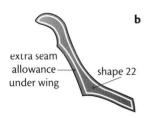

Trace and cut out freezer paper templates for shapes #21-24; on shape 21, keep the edge of the shape straight under the beak position. Assemble the robin body as shown in diagrams **c-h**. Start by ironing template 22 onto brown fabric; mark and cut it out in the usual way (**b**).

TIP: Allow extra seam allowance on the edge which is under the wing; this will ensure that the wing will cover the raw edges.

**6** Take the rust-coloured breast fabric and position shape 22 on top; use the plastic overlay to help identify the colour area which works best for the breast. Appliqué only the curved inner edge as shown (**c**).

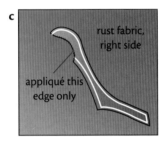 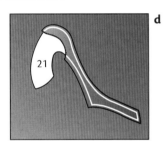

**7** Use the overlay to position template 21 on the rust fabric and iron it in place (**d**); keep the outer edge of template 21 correct with the overlay, even if the template doesn't perfectly match with the appliquéd seam. Iron the template in position and mark round it, then cut it out adding a seam allowance. Turn the work over to the reverse side and trim close to the seam stitched in step 6; this will separate the bird from the fabric (**e**). Trimming the construction seams means that the appliqué remains smooth and flat.

 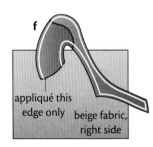

**8** Place the beige fabric under shape 21; check with the overlay that you will be able to position template 23 correctly later. Appliqué the lower edge of 21 to the fabric as shown (**f**).

**9** Use the overlay to position template 23 and iron it in place (**g**); again, keep the outer edge of the template correct with the overlay even if the template doesn't perfectly match the appliquéd seam. Mark round the template then cut out shape 23, adding a seam allowance. Turn the work over to the reverse side and trim close to the seam. You have now assembled the bird body as a complete unit (**h**), ready to transfer to the background.

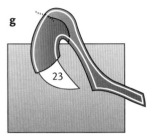 

**10** Use the main overlay to position the robin correctly on the background, and tack it down with small running stitches as usual. Appliqué the robin, changing thread colour as necessary. Where there are seams you will be able to turn both seam allowances under smoothly and so achieve a neat outline to the bird; this is an extra advantage of unit appliqué. Note that the edges which are covered by the wing are not turned under but left raw. Lastly, prepare the wing shape in the usual way and appliqué it in position.

## Embroidery

All the embroidery is worked with two strands of stranded embroidery thread except the ivy berries, which use three.

**11** Using grey-brown thread, embroider the robin's beak with straight stitches; use the same colour to embroider the legs, but this time using stem stitch. Add a French knot worked with black thread for the eye – or use a small bead.

**12** Embroider the twining ivy stem with two lines of stem stitch worked close together; stitch one line in dark brown and one in grey-brown.

**13** To help you keep a good shape to the clusters of ivy berries, use a white removable pen to draw ½in circles on the background as placement guides. Some groups of berries can be a little smaller, as shown on the design. The clusters of ivy berries are worked in French knots, using the two shades of light green embroidery thread; work with one strand of the paler tone and two strands of the deeper tone. (If you prefer, you could use beads instead of stitching French knots.) Your appliqué design is now complete.

## Finishing the quilt

### Assembling the quilt top

**14** Working with the design face down on a well-padded surface, press the appliqué carefully from the back. Trim the background to an accurate 12½in square.

**15** Trace templates A–E onto freezer paper and cut them out. Carefully mark points X, Y and Z, where the seams meet, and mark the straight grain lines on each template.

**16** Iron template A to the wrong side of the red border fabric (note that the straight grain is on the longest edge). Draw round the template to mark the stitching line, then cut out the shape adding a ¼in seam allowance all round; mark the matching points X, Y and Z. Cut out three more red triangles in the same way.

**17** Use the same technique to cut out two of each shapes B, C, D and E from the green outer border fabric; mark the matching points X, Y and Z.

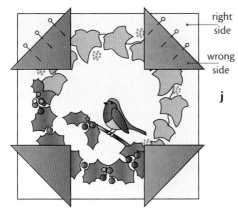

i

**18** On the centre block mark points X and Y on each side as shown (**i**), 3¾in from the corners and ¼in from the edge.

**19** Cut two 4⅜in squares from the red fabric, then cut each in half diagonally to make four triangles. (Cutting the triangles in this way means that the straight grain will be on the outer edge of the block when the triangles are stitched in position.) Use template A to mark points X and Y on each triangle. Position a triangle on

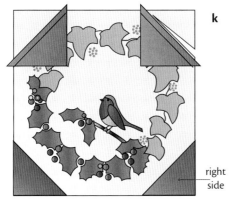

j

right side
wrong side

right side

k

each corner of the design, right sides together, matching points X and Y (**j**).

**20** Machine a ¼in seam on each triangle, and press the seam towards the triangle. Check that all the triangles are correctly positioned, then trim the seam allowance on the background fabric to ¼in (**k**).

**21** Assemble the side borders by stitching B and C to A as shown (**l**), matching points X, Y and Z carefully. Press the seams towards the triangles. Stitch an assembled border unit to opposite sides of the centre block (**m**). (Check that the triangle seams meet on the centre block before machining, and adjust if necessary.) Press the seams towards the border.

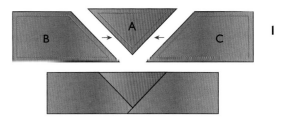

B          A          C          l

m

**22** Assemble the top and bottom borders in a similar way, but this time using D and E on each side of A (**n**). Stitch the top and bottom borders in place (**o**). Press the quilt top on the reverse side.

D          A          E

n

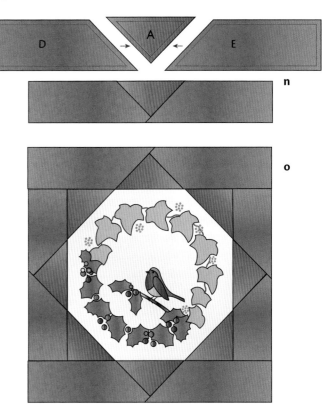

o

## Quilting

I used a combination of hand and machine quilting, as described below, but you could work all the quilting by hand or machine – whichever you prefer.

**23** In the centre of the wreath, use a hera to mark a diagonal ½in grid on the background. Follow the instructions on p122 to layer and prepare the quilt sandwich.

**24** Working a scant ⅛in from the edge of each appliqué shape, outline-quilt by hand the robin and the branch with its holly leaves. Use a fine thread to machine quilt the marked grid in the centre of the wreath.

**25** Outline-quilt by hand the remainder of the appliquéd leaves and berries. On all the leaves quilt centre vein lines, and quilt additional vein lines on the large ivy leaves. Quilting the vein lines gives more dimension to the leaves and helps them sit better on the background.

**26** Machine ¼in inside the border all around the centre block. Fill the space between this row of stitching and the appliqué with machine echo quilting.

**27** On each of the red triangles, mark round one of the smaller ivy leaf templates. Machine quilt the leaf outline and the centre vein – I used a gold thread. Use the large, medium and small ivy templates and arrange them attractively on one green border; machine quilt the leaf outlines and centre veins. Do the same on the other three borders to complete the quilting.

## Binding

**28** Trim the quilt to an accurate square. Cut binding strips 2⅜in wide. Join these to form a continuous double binding strip long enough to go round quilt plus extra for turning the corners and the final join; follow the instructions on p124 to bind the quilt.

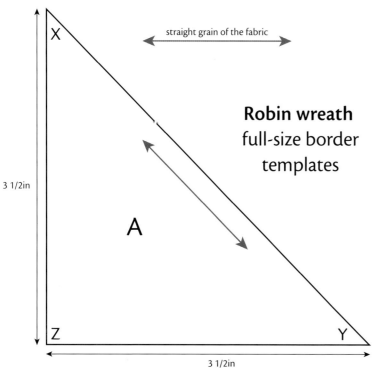

straight grain of the fabric

X

3 1/2in

A

Z

Y

3 1/2in

**Robin wreath**
full-size border
templates

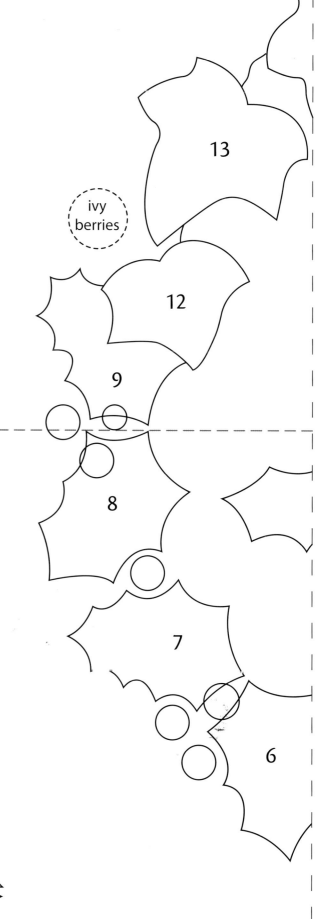

13

ivy
berries

12

9

8

7

6

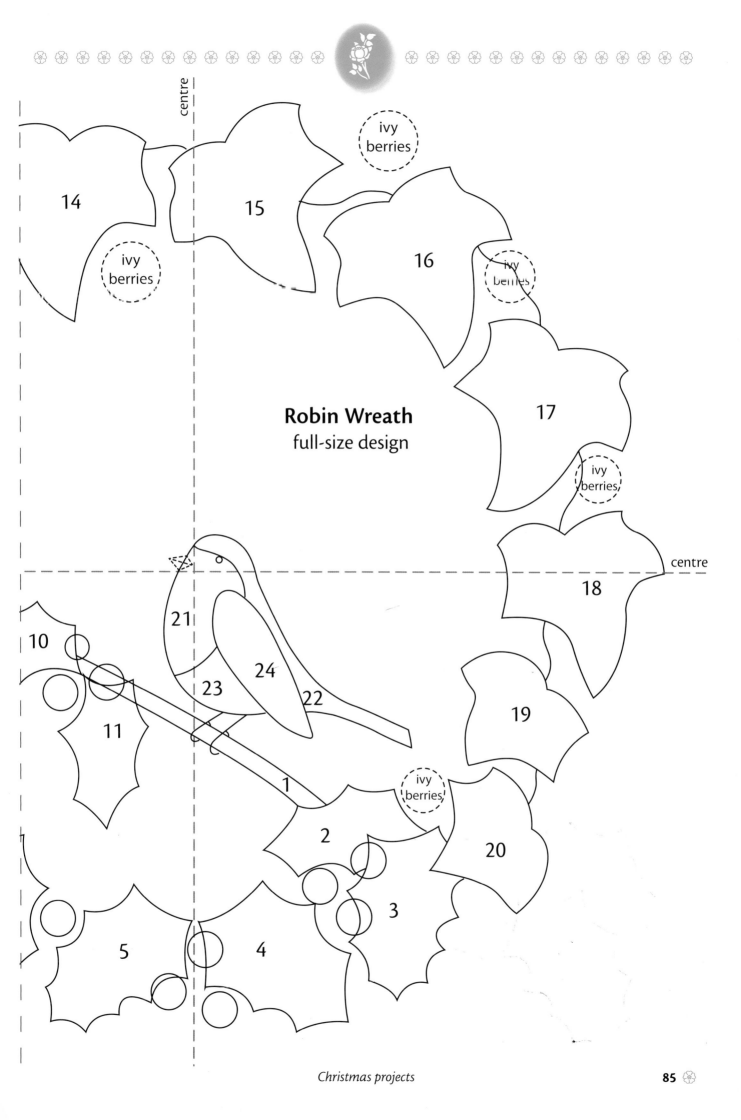

**Robin Wreath**
full-size design

centre

centre

14

15

ivy berries

ivy berries

16

ivy berries

17

ivy berries

18

21

24

10

23

22

11

19

1

2

ivy berries

20

3

5

4

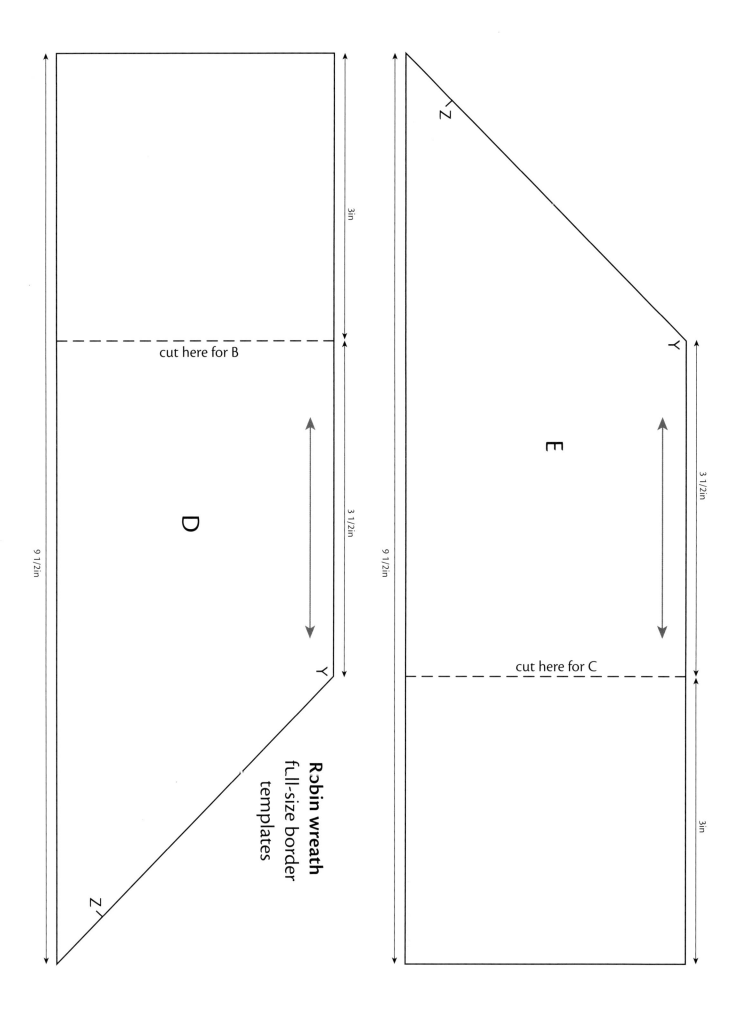

3in

cut here for B

D

3 1/2in

9 1/2in

Y

Z

**Robin wreath full-size border templates**

Z

Y

E

3 1/2in

9 1/2in

cut here for C

3in

## Project 8

# Robin Wreath 2

*This is a smaller version of the Robin Wreath design, worked 'on point' (at 45°) to make a mini wall-hanging. I stitched this version using machined raw-edge fused appliqué (see p23), which works well with these scaled-down shapes. Of course you could also use the same machine technique for the larger version, instead of needle turning as I described in the instructions on p80-82, but I don't recommend needle-turning this smaller version because of the smaller shapes. In this alternative design, I've quilted and bound the centre wreath block to make a mini quilt, which I then stitched on point to a background quilted square with pieced corners. Christmas fabrics with a touch of gold add a festive touch to the background quilt and the binding of both quilts.*

**Finished size:** *approx 12½in square*

## What you will need:

- 10in square of background fabric
- for the appliqué:
  - scraps of greens for the leaves
  - shaded red for the berries
  - brown, rust and beige for the robin
  - brown for the branch
- for piecing:
  - four 8in squares of dark green
  - scraps of red and green
- silk thread or alternative fine thread to match appliqué fabrics
- stranded embroidery thread, greyish/brown, black, rust, two tones of light green
- paper-backed fusible web
- freezer paper
- A4 size piece of thin, clear plastic such as an overhead projector or photocopier transparency
- for quilting the design:
  - low-loft wadding: 10in square for the wreath design plus 11½in square for the background quilt
  - backing fabric: 10in square for the wreath design plus 12in square for the background quilt
  - fine thread (eg YLI silk) to blend with the wreath background fabric
  - gold thread for quilting the pieced corners
- for binding: scraps of three dark/medium green fabrics, or ¼yd of dark green

## Preparation

**1**  Note that the design on p90-91 is given in reverse, so that all the templates are ready to trace for the fused appliqué technique. Make an overlay by tracing the design onto

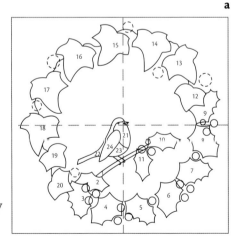

a

plastic, using a fine marker suitable for marking plastic; don't forget to mark the centre lines. Turn the tracing over (**a**), and use this reverse side of the overlay as a guide for placing the appliqué on the background.

**2**  Remember that the design is used on point, so fold the background fabric corner to corner and finger-press it to mark the centre; repeat with the other two corners.

Tack the centre lines for about 2in each side of the centre along the creased lines; you don't need to tack right across the design, and if you do the tacking might get fused under the appliqué.

**3**  Follow the instructions on p21 to prepare the holly and ivy leaves (templates #2–20) for fused appliqué; remember too to refer to the instructions on your specific product. It's a little trickier to fussy-cut with the fused technique, as you are working on the back of the fabric; if you would like to achieve a specific shading, especially on the ivy leaves, refer back to p15 for my method. When you are cutting out the prepared shapes, remember to allow a little extra on edges which are overlapped; this will ensure that there won't be any gaps between the shapes when they are fused in place on the background. The shapes are quite small, but it's still worth removing the fusible web from the centres of the shapes before fusing to the fabric to give a softer finish (see p21).

**4**  Prepare the branch (template #1) for fusing; allow extra fabric at each end to ensure that the raw edge will be covered by the leaves and berries.

**5**  Prepare the robin shapes using templates #21–24 on p90; note where a little extra has been added on the edges which will be underneath other shapes.

**6**  Cut a 2in square of fabric for the berries and back it with fusible web; use a circle template to mark 18 ¼in circles on the paper backing, and cut out the circles.

## Appliqué

**7**  Remove the paper backing from all the leaf and robin shapes, and from the branch. Position the reversed plastic overlay over the right side of the background fabric, matching the centres, and use it as a placement guide for the branch, ivy and holly leaves; slide each shape underneath and line it up with overlay. If you are using Steam-a-Seam™, the shapes can be finger-pressed in place for a temporary hold until they're permanently fused with the iron; if your fusible web doesn't have this facility, you may find it easier to arrange and fuse a few pieces at a time.

**8**  Assemble the robin shapes (21–24) on the background (**b**), using the overlay for accurate placement. (Again, if you aren't using Steam-a-Seam™ you'll find it easier to fuse one shape at a time.)

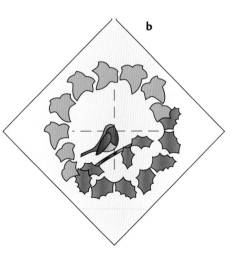

b

**9** Use a short straight machine stitch to stitch the branch and all the leaves in place, stitching close to the raw edges. Appliqué the robin in the same way, adding a few extra lines of stitching to the wing to suggest feathers.

**10** Remove the backing paper from the berries and fuse them in place as shown on the design. I didn't stitch these in place, but you could if you wished.

## Embroidery and quilting

**11** Follow the instructions for the main design to embroider the ivy stem, the ivy berries, and the robin's beak, legs and eye. Using one strand of rust-coloured embroidery thread, work a few straight stitches on the robin's breast.

**12** Use a hera to mark a grid of diagonal lines at ½in intervals in the centre of the wreath; mark diagonal lines in one direction only from the outer edge of the wreath to the outer edge of the background. Follow the instructions on p122 to layer the design with the 10in square of wadding and backing fabric; pin or tack/baste the layers together.

**13** All the quilting on this version is done by machine – if you basted the quilt, clip the threads and remove them as you quilt. Working a scant ⅛in from the appliqué patches, outline-quilt around the robin and the holly branch and its leaves. Quilt the marked grid in the centre. Outline-quilt the ivy leaves and the remaining holly leaves, then quilt the outer diagonal lines.

## Finishing

### Binding

**14** Trim the work to an accurate 9in square. Cut binding strips 1⅝in wide; you can either cut all of these from one piece of fabric or (as in my original) make the binding by joining strips of three different fabrics, each approximately 14in long. I think it's worth taking the extra trouble with a pieced binding as it gives a more subtle and interesting edge on this kind of small decorative quilt. The final binding strip needs to be long enough to fit around the quilt plus extra for corners and the final join.

> **TIP:** If there are several joins in the binding it's a good idea to place the binding round the quilt to see where the joins will come – you don't want joins to occur at the corners, so you may need to adjust the lengths of the strips to avoid this happening.

**15** Fold the strip in half to use as a double binding, and follow the instructions on p124 to bind the quilt (**c**), taking a ¼in seam.

### Making the background quilt

**16** Lay the 12in square of background fabric on a flat surface and position the 11½in square of wadding centrally on top. Pin the two layers together, and machine stitch the horizontal and vertical centre lines to attach the wadding to the backing. Tack the outer edge of the wadding to the backing fabric (**d**).

c

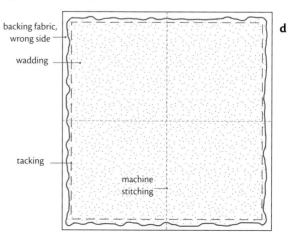

backing fabric, wrong side
wadding
tacking
machine stitching
d

**17** Cut two 3¼in squares from the dark green fabric; cut each in half diagonally to give you four triangles. Cut four 1 x 5½in strips of red fabric, four 1⅛ x 7in strips of green fabric and four 1⅛ x 8in strips of red fabric Take one strip of each fabric and piece to one green triangle as shown (**e**). Repeat with the remaining strips to make four pieced sections. Use a square ruler to trim each pieced section to make a 5¾in triangle (**f**).

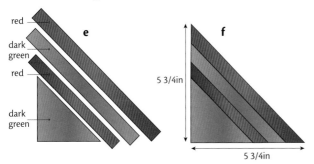

**18** Place one pieced triangle in each corner on top of the wadding (**g**); tack the edges of the triangles in position. Use gold thread to machine quilt down the centre of each red strip.

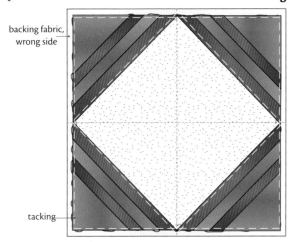

**19** Trim this background to an accurate square; cut binding strips and bind the quilt as described on p84 for the *Robin Wreath* block.

**20** Position the robin design centrally on the background quilt – the points will extend slightly over the edges of the background. Pin it in position. Slip-stitch in place ¼in under the binding, so that the very edge of the binding remains free of the background (**h**).

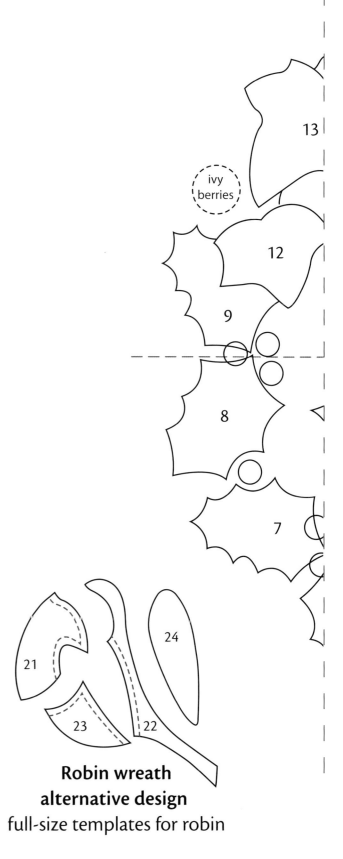

**Robin wreath
alternative design**
full-size templates for robin

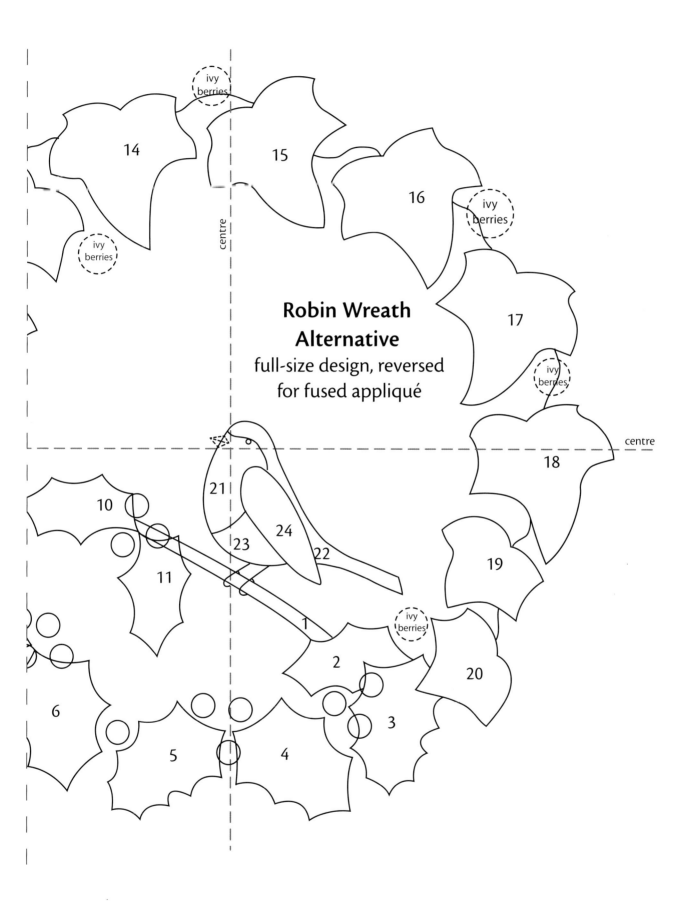

**Robin Wreath Alternative**
full-size design, reversed for fused appliqué

# Project 9

# Christmas Heart

*What could be more evocative of a traditional Christmas than this pretty heart-shaped wreath of holly, ivy and mistletoe, decorated with berries and baubles and tied with a shiny red ribbon bow? This project uses cut-away appliqué to stitch the mistletoe, and unit appliqué to assemble the bow. I stitched the original design using needle-turned appliqué, but it could equally well be stitched by machine using a small zigzag or buttonhole stitch to secure the appliquéd edges. Or you could mix and match techniques for different parts of the design. For example, you could use fused machine appliqué for the mistletoe, but needle-turn the leaves and bow. And how about using broderie perse for the ivy leaves if you can find a suitable leaf print? Refer back to the Appliqué Techniques section (p14-24) to help you select the methods that will work best for you – it's your choice!*

**Finished size:** *the design measures approx 11 x 12in*

## What you will need:

- 16in square background fabric
- for the appliqué:
  - small pieces of shaded reds for the bow and berries;
  - white/cream for the mistletoe berries
  - glitzy red/gold for the baubles;
  - dark green for the holly
  - mid green for the ivy (I fussy-cut a leaf print to get the shading on the ivy leaves)
  - 8in square of mid/light green for the mistletoe
- silk thread or alternative fine thread to match the appliqué fabrics
- freezer paper for templates
- stranded embroidery thread in dark green and brown

## Preparation

**1** Follow the instructions on p12 to mark the centre lines on the background with small tacking stitches. Make an overlay (see p12) and attach it to the background, then follow the instructions on p15 to make the freezer paper templates. Use templates #1-5 to prepare the holly leaves, and templates #6-16 to prepare the ivy leaves; fussy-cut the fabric to get interesting markings on the ivy leaves.

## Appliqué

### Leaves

**2** Appliqué the holly leaves (1-5) in numerical order, then do the same with the ivy leaves (6-16) as shown (**a**).

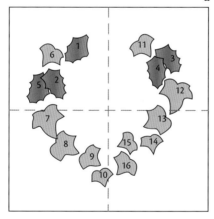

**3** As there are very narrow spaces between the shapes, which would make them difficult to needle-turn, the mistletoe stem (#22) and some of the mistletoe leaves are appliquéd using the cut-away appliqué technique (see p19). This isn't a problem, of course, if you choose to fuse the mistletoe in place. If you want to fuse it, simply trace off the whole mistletoe shape (reversed of course), including all the leaves, onto the back of the fusible web and proceed in the usual way (see p21). My approach was to appliqué some of the leaves (#17- 21) separately, but use the cut-away method for the stems with the remaining leaves attached. That is why template 22 is rather a strange shape!

**4** Cut a 4 x 7in rectangle of fabric for the mistletoe stems and put it to one side. From the remainder of the fabric prepare and cut out mistletoe leaves 17–21 in the usual way. I've suggested two ways to appliqué the separate mistletoe leaves. Either appliqué shapes 17-21 at this stage, using the overlay to position them accurately (**b**), or follow step 7 below and appliqué the leaves after completing the cut-away appliqué (steps 5 and 6). Whichever method you choose, you will need to appliqué leaf 21 at this stage. Leave raw edges at the top of the leaves and at the lower edge of shape 21.

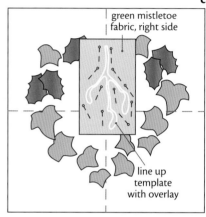

**5** Iron template 22 onto the right side of your reserved rectangle of green fabric. Mark round the shape with removable white pen, but keep the template in place. Place the rectangle of fabric onto the work, lining up the template with the overlay to position it correctly; pin securely (**c**), and remove the template.

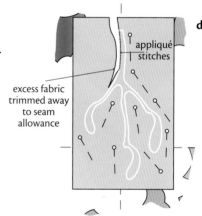

**6** Starting at the top of the main stem, cut away some of the fabric (leaving a small seam allowance) and start needle-turning the edge (**d**). As it becomes necessary, cut away a little more of the fabric, still leaving a seam allowance. Continue around the shape in the same way (**e**). If you have a problem matching the shape where it crosses the tops of the previously appliquéd leaves don't worry: note how strategically the berries are placed to cover any mismatch! Leave the seam allowance at the top of the mistletoe sprig raw, to be covered by the bow later.

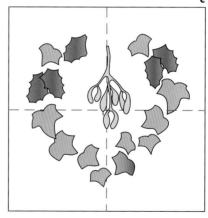

**7**  If you haven't already added leaves 17-20 at step 4, this is the time to do it. You could clip a stitch or two in the cut-away appliqué to that you can insert the tops of the leaves under shape 22 (**f**);

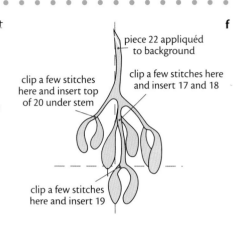

f

piece 22 appliquéd to background

clip a few stitches here and insert top of 20 under stem

clip a few stitches here and insert 17 and 18

clip a few stitches here and insert 19

these areas are covered by the berries (**g**), so it won't be a problem. Working on a well-padded surface, press the appliqué from the reverse.

g

### Bow

**8**  Unit appliqué is used to make the bow loops, using templates #23-28; this method will produce a smooth outer edge on the bow.

To make the first loop, choose a shaded fabric and use a window (see p15) to fussy-cut shape 24 – try to get the lighter area in the centre, with darker shading at the outer edge and near the centre knot (see photo **g**). This will give dimension to the bow. Mark around template 24 and add the registration marks (**h**).

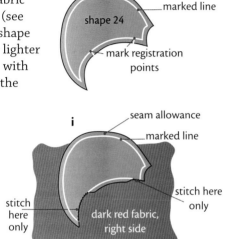

h

seam allowance

marked line

shape 24

mark registration points

i

seam allowance

marked line

stitch here only

stitch here only

dark red fabric, right side

Position shape 24 on a dark red fabric; appliqué only between the registration marks and the outer edges (**i**).

**9**  Use the plastic overlay to position template 23 in place (**j**) and draw round the inner and outer edges of the template (**k**). Cut out the assembled loop, adding a small seam allowance (**l**). Turn over the work to trim the little stitched seams and to add the seam allowance to the inner edge of 23 (**m**).

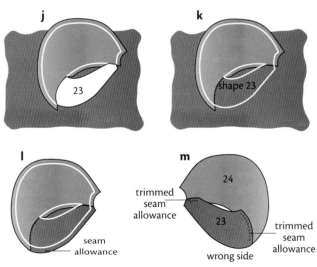

j

k

shape 23

23

l

m

24

trimmed seam allowance

23

seam allowance

trimmed seam allowance

wrong side

**10** Make the other loop of the bow in the same way using templates 25 and 26, and appliqué both loops to the background; the inner edges of the loops will need to be clipped in order to be able to turn the edges under (**n**),

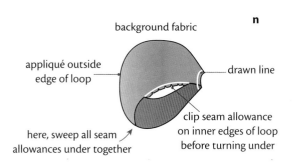

background fabric **n**

appliqué outside
edge of loop

drawn line

clip seam allowance
on inner edges of loop
before turning under

here, sweep all seam
allowances under together

## Embroidery

**12** Use two strands of brown embroidery thread and
work stem stitch to embroider the short lengths of ivy
stem as shown on the design. Use two strands of dark
green embroidery thread to embroider the sprigs of yew
using small straight stitches (**q** and **r**).

**r**

but the outer edges
are just stitched
in the usual way.
Appliqué the bow
ends (shapes 27
and 28). Finally
appliqué the bow
knot (shape 29),
which will cover up
all the raw edges in
the centre of the
bow (**o**).

**o**

### Berries

**11** Use the perfect circle method (see p20) to make the
berries; you will find the relevant circle templates on p127.
To make the mistletoe berries, cut out six ⅞in circles of
white or cream fabric and use a ⅜in card circle template;
appliqué the berries in position as shown in the main
photo. To make the holly berries cut out seventeen 1in

circles in a shaded
red fabric and use a
½in circle template
(I made one or two
of the berries a
little smaller to give
variety). A shaded
red works better
than a plain red,
which can make
the design look
a little spotty. To
make the baubles
cut out seven 1⅛in
circles of a red/gold
fabric and use a ⅝in
circle template –
again I made some
a little smaller to
fit better into the
spaces between the
leaves. Appliqué
the berries and
baubles in position
(**p**) as shown on the
design.

**p**

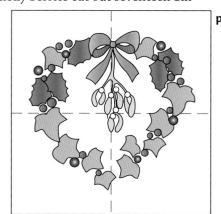

**q**

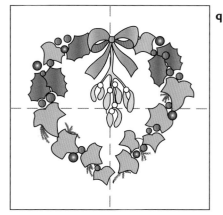

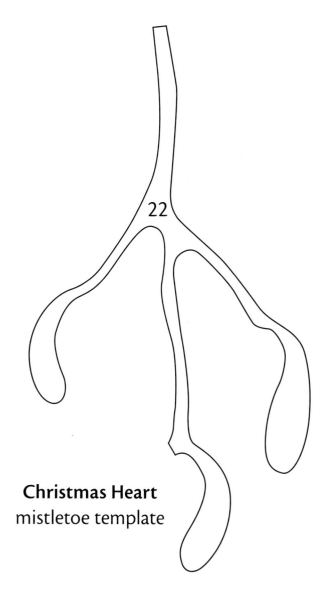

22

## Christmas Heart
mistletoe template

# Christmas Heart
## full-size design

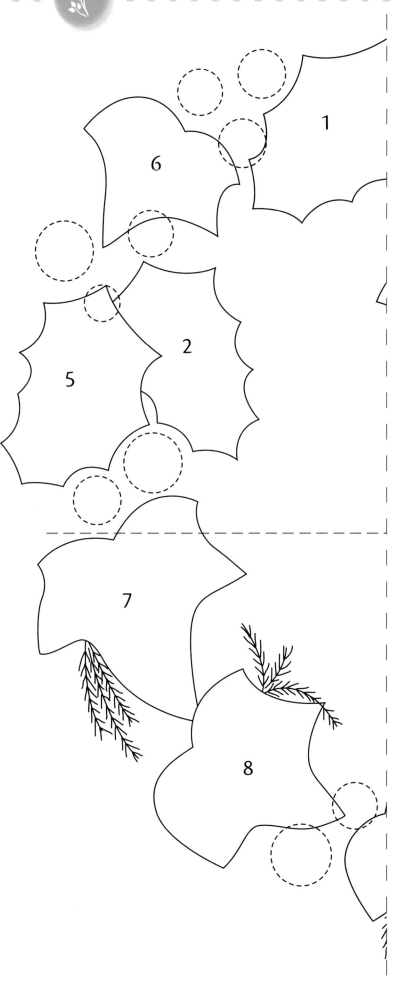

position of
berries/baubles

*Christmas projects*

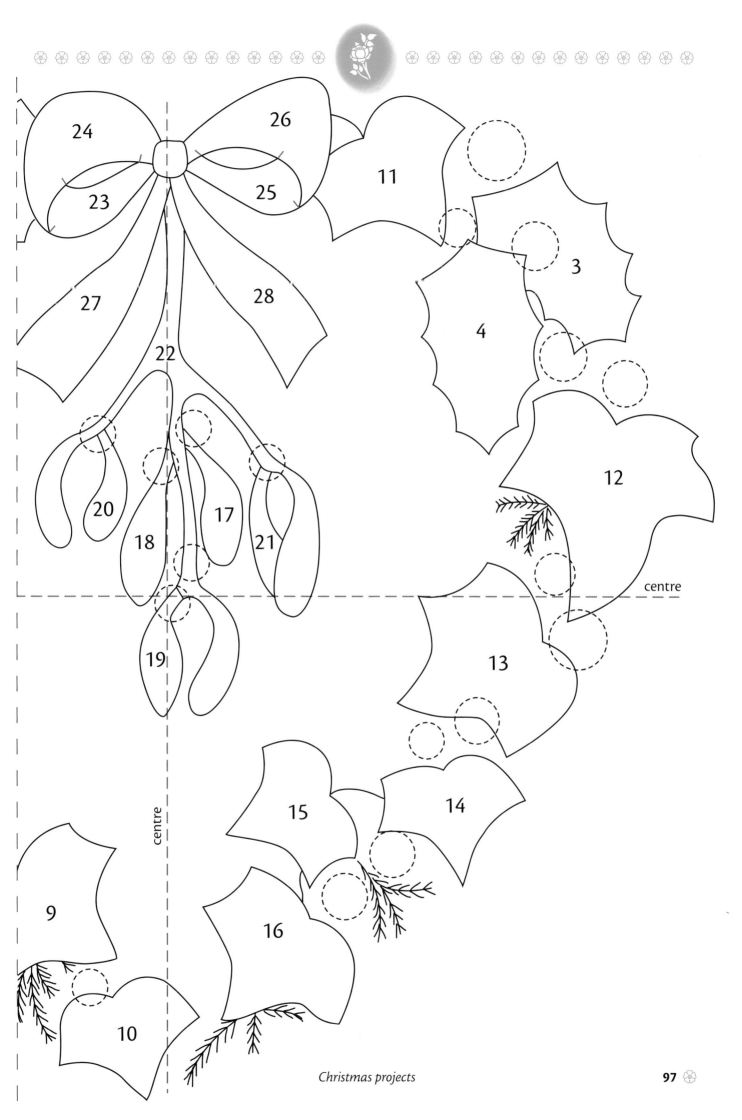

24

26

23

25

11

27

28

22

3

4

20

17

18

21

12

19

centre

13

15

14

9

16

centre

10

*Christmas projects*

# Lined appliqué

## Lining shapes

When you are using very light-coloured fabrics for appliqué – especially when you're working on a coloured background – it can work very well to line the appliqué shapes. Lining them prevents both the background colour and the turned-under seam allowances from showing through on the front of the work; it also gives more 'body' to the appliquéd piece. A lightweight cotton fabric can be used for the lining; this could be white, or could be the same fabric that you're using for the appliqué shape. For a more padded look, you can use a low-loft wadding such as Thermore™.

There are several ways in which to line appliqué – choose the method which best suits the particular design you're doing and the fabrics you're using. The basic method is to cut the lining slightly smaller than the appliqué shape (Method One steps 1 and 2). Use an overlay to position the lining shape on the background, then tack it in position ¼in from the edge so that the seam allowance of the appliqué shape can be tucked under the lining. This method works well for larger shapes, but is difficult with small shapes which cannot easily be tacked. Here are three methods I developed for using with small pieces such as in the *Daisy* designs – *Daisy Meadow* cushion (p100) and *A Really Useful Bag* (p106).

### Method 1

In this method, the lining shape is fused to the background fabric.

**1** To make the appliqué template, trace the appliqué shape onto the matt side of freezer paper and cut it out leaving a 'window'. Number the template and the window (**a**).

**2** To make the lining, place the window on your chosen lining fabric and draw round the inside edge of the window (**b**).

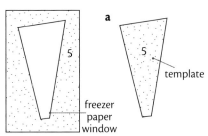

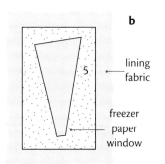

Cut out the lining shape (**c**); using this method, the lining will be slightly smaller than the final appliqué piece – which is what you want!

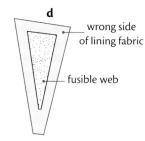

**3** Cut a small piece of paper-backed fusible web to fit the back of the lining shape, keeping it at least ⅛in inside the edges. This piece doesn't have to be cut exactly to the original shape – it just needs to be big enough to hold the shape in the centre. Iron the web side of this piece onto the back of the lining shape, and remove the paper backing (**d**).

**4** Use the overlay (see p12) to position the lining shape on the background. (Ensure that the shape is web-side-down on the background fabric, otherwise it will stick to the iron and not the fabric!) Fuse the lining in place (**e**).

**5** Using the overlay as a placement guide, position the prepared appliqué shape on the background; place the pins in the seam allowance. Remove the freezer paper template, then appliqué the shape in position, turning the seam allowance under the lining shape.

> **TIP:** If you're working with white or very pale fabrics, a white marked line doesn't show up well. I prefer not to use a coloured marker in case the line isn't fully removable. However, I have found that a small hera (see p10) works well for marking the turning line; it creates a sharp crease which shows up well. It's particularly good for geometric shapes and fairly straight lines; on a more complex shape, keep the template ironed in position on the appliqué shape and don't mark round the shape at all – use the edge of the template as the guide for turning the seam allowance. Usually though you can see the lining through the appliqué fabric (which is the reason for lining it!), and this will give you a guide for needle-turning the edges.

## Method 2

For this method, the lining shape is tacked to the reverse of the appliqué shape. Follow steps 1 and 2 for Method 1 (above), then proceed as follows:

**1**  Use running stitch to stitch the lining shape to the reverse of the appliqué fabric; cut out the shape, adding the usual seam allowance (**a**).

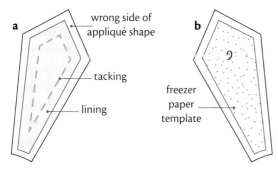

**2**  Use a hera to mark round the lining on the wrong side (this will produce a crease on the right side), or iron the freezer paper template in place on the right side to use as a guide for the turning line (**b**), as suggested in the TIP, above.

**3**  Position the prepared shape on the background, using the overlay for placement; appliqué the shape in position as for Method 1, turning the seam allowance under the lining.

## Method 3

For Method 3, the lining shape is fused to the reverse of the appliqué shape. Begin by following step 1 for Method 1, then proceed as follows:

**1**  Cut a piece of paper-backed fusible web a little bigger than the appliqué shape. Cut a piece of lining fabric slightly larger than the piece of fusible web, and iron the web to the lining fabric. To create the lining shape, place the freezer paper window on the paper backing of the web

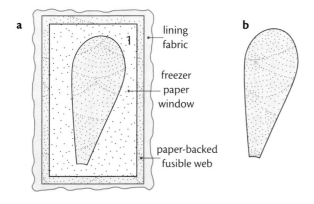

(**a**) and draw round the inside edge of the window. Cut out the lining shape (**b**) and remove the paper backing.

**2**  Fuse the lining shape to the wrong side of the appliqué fabric (**c**). (Ensure that the piece is placed web-side-down on the appliqué fabric – otherwise the lining will stick to the iron and not the fabric! It's not always easy to see

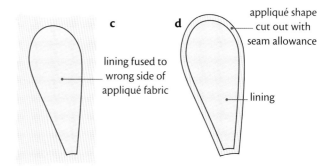

the web adhesive on white fabrics …) Cut out the shape, adding the usual seam allowance (**d**).

**3**  Mark round the edge of the lining shape with a hera to produce a crease as a guide for needle-turning, or simply turn the edge using the lining as a guide (the lining gives you a firm edge against which to turn). I find that using the firm edge of the lining is particularly helpful when sewing curved edges; I chose this method for the daisy appliquéd to the *Really Useful Bag* project.

**4**  Position the prepared shape on the background, using the overlay as a placement guide; place the pins in the seam allowance, and appliqué as usual (**e**). The fused lining gives a slightly raised effect to the appliqué, and produces a crisp finish. I used this technique for the clematis flowers in *Spring Basket* (p112), shown in the close-up photo below.

TIP: Here's a speedy technique if you have several pieces to line. I say 'speedy' rather tongue-in-cheek, as lining is an additional step in hand appliqué! However, with a little organisation you can speed up the process. Take a piece of lining fabric big enough to line all the pieces you need; back it with a piece of fusible web cut slightly smaller than the fabric. Trace all the lining shapes onto the paper backing of the fusible web, using the windows as guides; number the shapes as on the design. Cut out the shapes as needed and fuse them to the back of the prepared appliqué shapes.

## Project 10

# *Daisy Meadow*

*The inspiration for this design was a daisy-filled sunny meadow. The white and light-coloured daisy flowers are an opportunity to practise some of the lined appliqué techniques we discussed on p98-99; and of course you can use brighter colours which may not then need lining. The stylized flowers are in three basic styles in various sizes. The petals tips are either straight, pointed or rounded, so there's plenty of scope for perfecting points and curves.*

*Even though the appliqué fabrics are very light in colour, it's worth choosing a patterned print or shaded batik to create some subtle shading on the flowers. I pieced the background using five tones of green print fabric to suggest the meadow; I strip-pieced leftover fabric for the back of the cushion. In my original the appliqué is needle-turned, but the design would work well in machined appliqué too. The basic flower shapes are very versatile and can be incorporated into other projects; for example, I appliquéd a large daisy on the front of the bag shown on p107.*

**Finished size:** *the cushion measures approx 17½in square*

## What you will need:

- for the pieced cushion front, five tones of green cotton fabric (a fat eighth of each tone will be enough for the front)
- ⅝yd green fabric for the cushion back – this will also allow you sufficient for the piping and to use as one of the green fabrics for front. Alternatively you could piece the back too, using fabric left over from the front.
- for the appliqué:
  - small pieces of white prints, and shaded pinks in light and medium tones, for the daisies
  - various tones of shaded yellow and orange for the daisy centres
  - small piece of white lightweight cotton to line the daisies
- silk thread or alternative fine thread to match the appliqué fabrics
- freezer paper for templates
- for quilting the cushion front:
  - 20in square low-loft wadding
  - 20in square backing fabric
  - machine quilting thread
- 14in zip
- 2½yd narrow piping cord

## Preparation

**1**  Refer to the layout diagram (p104) to see where the different tones of background fabrics are placed. Label your background fabrics 1–5, with the lightest tone being 1 and the darkest 5.

Cut out squares and strips for the pieced background as follows:

| fabric | 3½in square | 5½in square | 1½ x 5½in strip | 1½ x 6½in strip |
|---|---|---|---|---|
| 1 | 2 | 1 | | |
| 2 | | 1 | 2 | 1 |
| 3 | 3 | 2 | 1 | 2 |
| 4 | 2 | 2 | 1 | 1 |
| 5 | 5 | | 2 | 2 |

I actually cut the squares which were to be appliquéd ½in bigger, ie 4in and 6in respectively, and trimmed them to the correct size after stitching the appliqué. This is because the appliqué may shrink or distort the background a little during stitching. After you've finished the appliqué, press the squares and trim them to sizes given in the cutting chart, keeping the appliqué centrally placed on each one.

**2**  Trace each daisy (A–E) onto a piece of tracing paper, greaseproof paper or plastic, so that you have an overlay for each style of daisy.

## Appliqué

Your choice of appliqué fabric and background colour will determine whether you get any show-through of the background or seam allowances, and therefore whether you need to line the appliqué shapes. Generally white fabric shapes will look better if they're lined. You could use any of the three lining methods described on p98-99 to line the daisies; however Method 3 (fusing the lining onto the reverse of the appliqué shape) is best for the round-petalled daisies.

As there are lots of small, similar shapes which may need lining it pays to be organised with the templates and the linings. The instructions which follow here refer to daisy A, but all the daisies are made in the same way.

**1**  To make the templates, take a strip of freezer paper and trace off the petal shapes (templates #1–9) for daisy A. Number each petal and its corresponding window, and cut out the templates (**a**). Keep the templates and windows for each daisy in a separate small plastic bag; some of the templates are used more than once. Daisy A is used twice, B three times, D twice and E four times; the templates can be re-used if they haven't been mislaid!

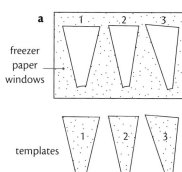

**2**  Use the window to mark out the lining shapes on the lining fabric (**b**) (or on the paper backing of the fusible web if you are using Method 3). Cut out each lining and pin it to a numbered piece of paper so that it's easy to identify each one (**c**); if you mark directly onto the fabric lining this may show through the appliqué later. (If you are using method 3, you can write on the paper backing as the paper is removed later.)

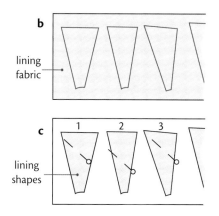

**3**  Crease each square diagonally to find the centre (or judge it by eye). To position the overlay, use a pin through the centre dot to line up with the centre of the fabric square.

*Lined appliqué*     **101**

**6** For the centre of the flower, cut out a 1¼in diameter circle of fabric (see circle templates on p127); use a ¾in diameter card or Mylar™ circle template, and follow the instructions on p20 to create the centre. Appliqué the fabric circle in position (**h**) using a slightly different appliqué stitch. Run the needle under the folded outer edge of the circle, taking a small stitch before inserting the needle into the background. Take a small stitch in the background before bring the needle back up under the edge of the circle. Continue in this way around the circle, keeping a smooth outer edge to the shape.

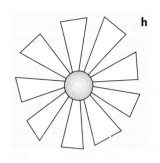

**7** Appliqué all the daisies in a similar way, using the appropriate templates and circle sizes for the centres. Working on a well-padded surface, press all the appliquéd squares from the back. Trim them if necessary so that the small patches measure 3½in square and the large patches are 5½in square.

## Assembling the cushion front

To piece the background, use a ¼in seam allowance; follow the steps below, and refer back to the layout diagram on p104 at each step so that the pieces are joined in the correct order. Press all the seams to one side.

**8** Join a 5½in strip to one side of each large square (**i**). (Refer to the layout diagram if you want to be specific about the orientation of your daisy, but the daisies can be used any way round.)

**9** Join the 3½in squares in pairs (**j**), then join the paired squares to the large squares (**k**). You will now have six units – keep referring to the layout diagram to check that you're assembling the units correctly.

**10** Join a 6½in strip to each of the top units (**l**), and a 6½in strip to each of the lower units (**m**). Press the

**4** Iron freezer paper templates 1–9 onto the right side of the appliqué fabric. Cut the shapes out, adding the usual seam allowance (and make sure that you add a generous allowance at the base of each petal). Prepare the lining according to your chosen method chosen, then use the overlay to position petals 1, 3, 5 and 7; appliqué the petals in position (**d**). (It's easier to appliqué alternate petals as you work round the daisy, as the petals are quite close to each other in the centre.)

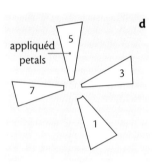

**5** Line up the overlay with the appliquéd petals and position petals 2, 4, 6 and 8; appliqué these petals in position (**e**). Finally appliqué petal 9 (**f**).

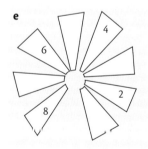
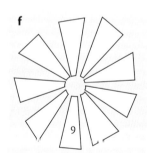

TIP: some of the petals are quite narrow at the base. After stitching the first side of each petal, lift the petal and trim the seam allowance close on the stitched side. Place the petal back in the original position and continue with the appliqué (g).

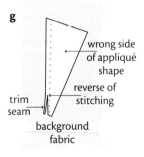

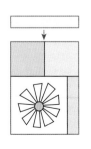
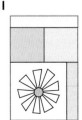

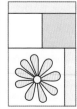

seams towards the large squares and away from the small squares; this allows the seam allowances to butt up when the pieced strips are joined later.

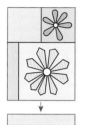 m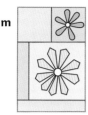

lower row of units

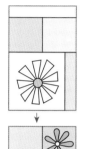 n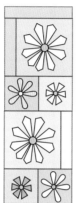

o

**11** Join the top and lower units in pairs (**n**) to form three strips; press the seams towards the large squares and away from the small squares. Finally, join the pieced strips (**o**) to complete the pieced cushion front as shown in the layout diagram.

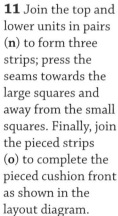 

## Finishing

### Quilting

**12** Trim the work to an accurate square. Working on a cutting mat, use a hera (see p10) to mark diagonal lines 1in apart, working out from the centre. Be careful not to mark across the appliqué – it's very difficult to remove the crease. Alternatively you could machine quilt in-the-ditch around the squares.

**13** Follow the instructions on p122 to layer the cushion front, wadding and backing fabric to make a quilt sandwich. Outline-quilt the daisies using a regular cotton sewing thread. Alternatively you could use bold quilting as on the *Leafy Tree* (p30); this would work well if you choose to quilt in-the-ditch around the squares instead of diagonal quilted lines.

**14** Quilt the diagonal lines by hand or machine (the original was hand quilted).

### Assembling cushion cover

**15** Trim the cushion front to an accurate square – the quilting will have slightly reduced it. Make the cushion back the same size as the front; it can either be made from all one fabric, or pieced from strips left over from the front. I did the latter and inserted a zip into one of the seams (**p**). Even if you are not piecing the back, cut the back in two sections, adding seam allowances; insert the zip in the seam.

p

**16** I piped the edge of the cushion; if you would like to do the same, follow the instructions in *Finishing Techniques* p125. If you prefer, omit the piping and simply place the front and back together, right sides facing. Pin the edges together, matching the raw edges; undo the zip a little. Stitch around the outer edge, taking a ¼in seam; clip the corners, slide open the zip, and turn the cover to the right side.

| 2 | 5 | 3 |

| 5 | 3 | 5 | 4 | 1 | 5 |

Daisy B
white

| 1 | 4 | | | 2 | 3 |

Daisy A
white

| 5 | 3 |

Daisy E
pale pink

Daisy D
white

Daisy C
pink

| 4 | 5 | 3 | 2 | 3 | 1 |

Daisy E
pink

Daisy E
white

Daisy B
white

| 5 | 3 | | | 4 | 2 |

Daisy B
pale pink

| 4 | 5 |

Daisy D
pink

Daisy E
white

Daisy A
pale pink

| 4 | 3 | 5 |

1 lightest tone     2 light/medium tone     3 medium tone     4 medium/dark tone     5 darkest tone

*Lined appliqué*

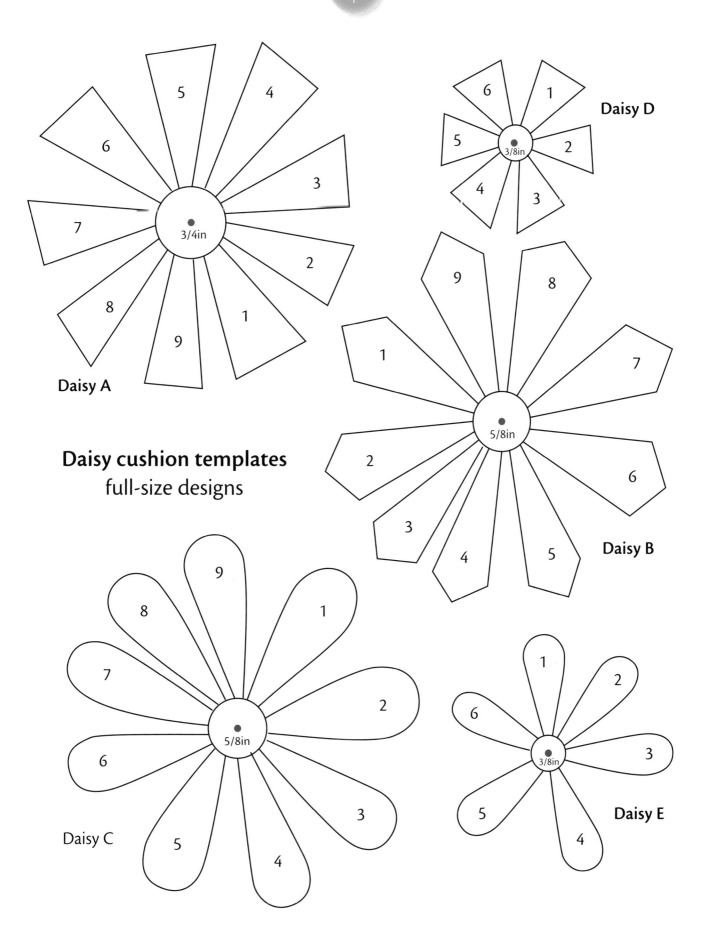

**Daisy A**

**Daisy cushion templates**
full-size designs

**Daisy D**

**Daisy B**

**Daisy C**

**Daisy E**

# Project 11

# A Really Useful Bag

*I've been using this handy little bag constantly for the past year and have found it a really useful size, especially when I'm travelling. A purse, glasses, book, mobile phone and small bottle of water fit neatly inside, and it encourages me not to carry round too much unnecessary clutter! The bag handles are just the right length for wearing the bag on the shoulder with the bag neatly under the arm, which also keeps your possessions safer. Other useful style features are the little side loops, which you can clip items to, and the flat base which keeps the bag upright.*

*I used Japanese woven fabrics and prints for a neutral, subtle look which goes with both summer and winter outfits. Of course, though, you can choose whatever colours you prefer. The bag is strip-pieced, but you could vary the piecing using different sized strips or squares, or make the bag from just one piece of fabric. I've appliquéd a large, simple daisy on the front of the bag, but how about pinning on one of the dimensional roses (p39) instead? I pinned one to the back of the bag to give you an idea of how this might look, as shown on p111.*

*Although the original was hand appliquéd, the daisy could easily be machine appliquéd. I used a zip fastening for extra security but you could use magnetic catches or fabric ties instead, which would be a little easier to sew. So there is plenty of scope for personalising and adapting the bag to meet your needs. Enjoy creating your own 'really useful bag.'*

**Finished size:** *The bag measures approx 10in square; the base is 2in wide*

## What you will need:
❀ for the bag:
- two Japanese woven fabrics, one dark (fabric A) and one light (fabric B)
- two Japanese prints, one dark (fabric C) and one light (fabric D)
- (you need less than a fat quarter of each fabric) (see cutting list)

❀ for the daisy appliqué:
- small pieces of cream print
- scrap of dull gold fabric
- small piece of white lightweight cotton to line the shapes
- silk thread or alternative fine thread to match the daisy fabrics

❀ machine stitching thread for piecing and making up bag

❀ freezer paper for templates

❀ scrap of fusible web (for lining the daisy)

❀ for the quilting

- 12 x 28in low-loft wadding
- 12 x 28in lining fabric
- machine quilting thread to outline-quilt the daisy

❀ 10in zip

❀ 50in of cord for the handles (lengthen or shorten these if you prefer)

## Preparation
**1** Cut the following pieces for the different sections of the bag.

For the bag front:
> from fabric A, one piece 5½ x 11in
> from fabric B, one piece 4½ x 11in
> from fabric D, one piece 2 x 11in

For the bag back:
> from fabric A, one piece 4 x 11in and one piece 2 x 11in
> from fabric B, one piece 4 x 11in and one piece 1½ x 11in
> from fabric D, one piece 1½ x 11in

For the base:

from fabric A, one piece 11 x 3½in.

For the handles:

from fabric C cut 1¼in bias strips; join these to give you a total length of 30in for each handle. (Before you cut the bias strips, check the width of the strip against the thickness of your cord; you may need to cut you bias wider.)

For binding:

from fabric A, cut a bias strip 2¼ x 24in for the top edge

from fabric C, cut a bias strip 2¼ x 25in for the bottom edge.

## Making the bag

Use a ¼in seam allowance unless stated otherwise.

### Piecing the front and back

**2** Join the strips together to assemble the bag front as shown (**a**); press the seams open.

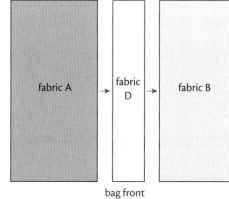

| fabric A | fabric D | fabric B |

bag front

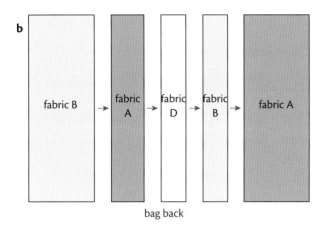

| fabric B | fabric A | fabric D | fabric B | fabric A |
|---|---|---|---|---|

bag back

Join the strips together to assemble the bag back as shown (**b**), and press the seams open.

## Appliqué

**3** Trace and cut freezer paper templates #1–9 for the daisy petals, and prepare these for appliqué. Whether you will get see-through of the background and seam allowances depends on the colour of the appliqué daisy fabric; generally white/cream fabrics are better for being lined. If you do need to line the daisy use Method 3 on p99, as this method helps to keep a smooth edge on the rounded petals. If you don't need to line the petals, prepare the fabric shapes as usual.

**4** Position the flower centrally on the bag front, about 4¾in up from base; refer to the *Daisy Meadow* project (p100) for tips on how to appliqué the daisy. Cut a 1⅛in circle from the dull gold fabric for the flower centre; use a ⅝in plastic/card circle to prepare the fabric circle (see p20) and appliqué it in the centre of the daisy (**c**).

## Quilting

**5** Cut two 12in squares of lining fabric and two 12in squares of wadding. Layer both the bag front and the bag back with the wadding and lining to make two quilt 'sandwiches;' secure the layers with safety pins (see p122). To prepare the base for quilting, cut a piece of wadding 11 x 3½in and a piece of lining the same size. Layer the base fabric with wadding and lining and secure the layers with safety pins.

**6** Outline-quilt the daisy petals (**d**). On the bag front and back sections, quilt the seams in the ditch, then add additional quilting as you wish on the back of the bag; I worked extra lines of quilting in the centre of the wide dark strip, and diagonal lines across the wide light strip.

**7** On the base section quilt diagonal lines, 1¼in apart. Trace and cut out the base template (template A), then pin this to right side of the quilted base section and cut out the shape (¼in seam allowance is included).

**8** Trim the back and front bag sections to accurate 11in squares. Tack round the edges of the front, back and base pieces to keep the layers together as you assemble the bag.

## Assembling the bag

**9** To make the side loops, cut a piece 2 x 1¼in from fabric A and a second piece, the same size, from fabric B. On the long edges of each piece, fold the raw

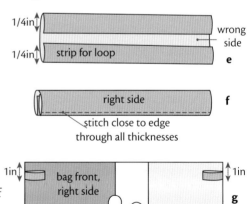

edges over by ¼in to the wrong side (**e**). Fold each strip in half along its length and machine or hand stitch edges together (**f**). Fold each loop in half and position one on each side of the bag front, with the base of the loop 1in from the top edge and all the raw edges together (**g**).

**10** Place the front and back sections together, right sides facing, and stitch the side seams (by doing this the loops will be stitched into the seam). The seam can be neatened in either of two ways; you could zigzag the raw edges together, but I preferred to neaten the seams by covering them with an extra strip of lining fabric. To do this, first

*Lined appliqué*

press the seams open. Cut two strips of lining fabric each 11 x 1¼in; press a ¼in turning to the wrong side along each of the long edges. Pin a strip over each seam and slip stitch the folded edges to the bag lining (**h**).

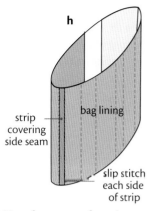

**11** On the lower edge of the bag, use pins to mark the centre front and centre back. Mark the centres on the base as shown by points W, X, Y and Z on base template A. Pin the base in position on the bag with the *wrong* sides facing, matching the centre points; the side seams of the bag should match points Y and Z on the base. Pin at right angles to the edge, easing the fabric round the curved ends (**i**). Try to keep the seam allowance even all the way round, so pin well round the curves; you may need to make a few clips in the seam allowance of the bag at the

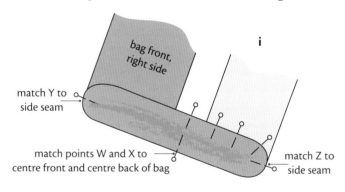

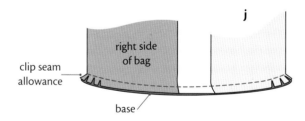

curves to help it stretch round the base shape (**j**). Stitch the base in place using a ¼in seam; note that the stitching is on the right side of the bag.

**12** Neaten the base seam with a double binding. Cut a bias strip 2¼in wide and long enough to go round the base plus extra for joining – so don't cut the strip to length until you've made the join. Fold the bias strip in half, *wrong* sides together. Open up the start of the binding strip and fold it back as shown (**k**), then re-fold the strip in half. Pin the binding on the right side of the bag, keeping the edge of the bias strip level with the lower edge of the bag; start in the centre of the bag where the

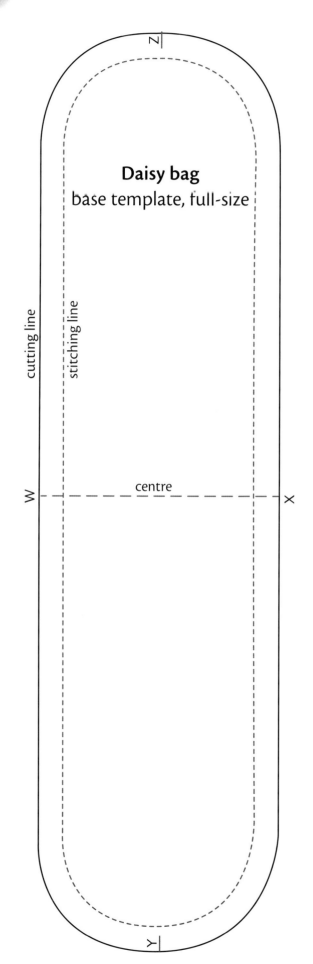

*Lined appliqué*

edge is straight (**l**). Pin all the way around and overlap the beginning of the binding strip by 2in. Trim off the excess binding strip and tuck the end tail inside the start of the binding

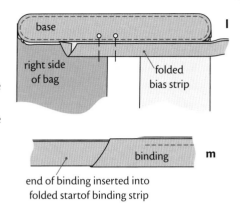

(**m**). Stitch the binding in place, taking a ¼in seam – you may find it helpful to tack the binding firmly in position but still keep the pins in, as you are stitching through several layers and dealing with the curved edges. To complete the binding, turn the binding strip over the raw edges to the base and pin; hem in place to the machine stitching line for a neat finish.

**13** Take the bias strip you've cut for binding the top edge of the bag and fold it in half, *wrong* sides facing, to make a double binding. On the right side, pin, join and machine stitch the binding in place around the top edge of the bag as in step 12 above, but don't turn the binding over to the inside yet.

**14** Place the zip centrally inside the top of the bag, with one tape ⅛in below the back top edge and the opposite tape ⅛in below the front top edge (**n**); fold under the ends of the tapes to neaten them. Tack the zip in place and then machine stitch ⅛in from the edge of the tape to secure the zip in place. (Note that this stitching will be on top

of the stitching used to secure the binding in place.) To complete the binding, turn the binding strip over the raw edges to the inside of the

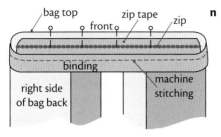

bag and pin it to the zip tape; for a neat finish, hem it in place to the machine stitching on the zip tape.

**15** To make the handles, fold each 30in bias strip in half, right sides facing, and machine a ¼in seam down the length of the strip. Turn the strips to the right side. A loop turner is useful for turning, or you could use the following technique. Put a loop of thread in a large darning needle and secure this thread firmly at the top of the strip (**o**). Drop the needle, eye first, down inside the strip, and push it along to pull the strip inside out.

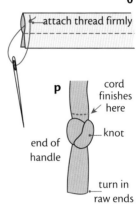

**16** Cut a 25in length of cord for each handle; the cord needs to be 2½in shorter than the handle at each end. Fasten a small safety pin on one end of the cord, and thread it through the handle strip. Use a single overhand knot to tie the handle at each end of the cord, then turn in ¼in of fabric at the ends and neatly oversew the turnings to close them (**p**).

**17** Position the handles on the bag, 2½in from each side and with the knot 1½in below the top edge of bag (**q**). Stitch the handles firmly to the bag from the knot to the binding, stitching right through to the lining. Leave the end below the knot hanging free.

## Daisy bag design
## full-size templates

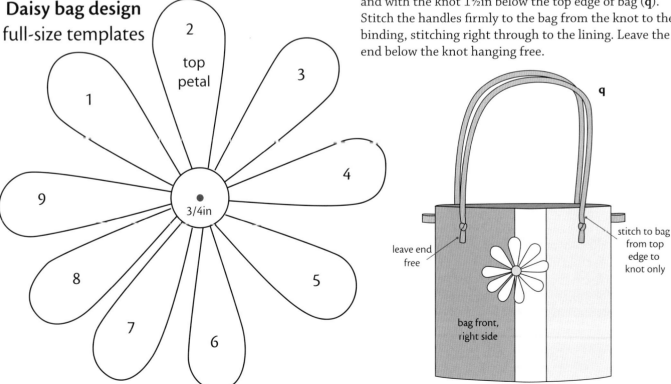

*Lined appliqué*

# *Really Useful Bag Variations*

*The main instructions describe the way I made my original Really Useful Bag, but as I suggested in the project introduction there are many ways in which you could adapt the construction or design. Here are ten suggestions; I'm sure you can think of lots of other ways of making the design your own!*

## Handles

• *Make wider, flat handles. Cut strips 2½in wide x the desired length; fold each strip in half lengthways, right sides facing, and stitch a ¼in seam, leaving a 3in gap halfway along for turning (a). Turn the handle so that the seam lies centrally down the middle, and press the seam open. Machine a ¼in seam across each end of handle (b); turn to right side through the opening and press. Slip stitch the gap closed. Machine stitch the strip ⅛in inside each edge.*

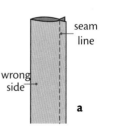
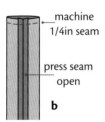

• *Use a decorative purchased cord instead of fabric strips for the handles.*

## Fastening

• *Create fabric ties instead of using a zip to close the top of the bag. Make the ties in the same way as for the side loops (step 9 above), cutting the strips to your chosen length.*

• *Fasten the top of the bag with a button and a loop instead of a zip.*

• *Use a magnetic fastening for the top.*

## Base

• *If you don't want to bind the lower edge of the bag, stitch the base in place with the fabrics right sides together, so that the seam is on the inside, then neaten the seam inside with a zigzag stitch.*

• *If you wish, you can omit the separate base. This method makes an integral base and is easier to stitch than creating a separate base. Cut the bag front and back sections 1in longer than specified in the main instructions, then join the bottom edges of the quilted front and back (a). Zigzag the seam to neaten it, then stitch the side seams and neaten them. Re-fold the base of the bag as shown (b); flatten the base, with the seam line running centrally. Draw the seam line AB (this should measure ¾in each side of the side seam line) and machine the marked seam.*

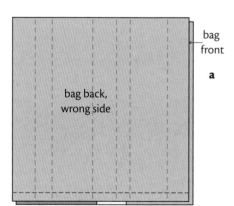

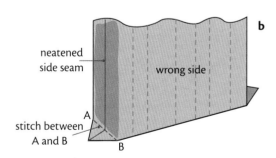

## Features

• *Position the side loops inside the bag – useful for clipping keys safely inside.*

• *Appliqué a different motif (leaves from the Leafy Tree perhaps), by either hand or machine.*

• *Add a dimensional flower.*

# The Grand Finale

## Project 12

# Spring Basket

*I've included some of my favourite spring flowers in an elegant woven basket for the final project. The design includes many of the techniques which have been covered so far in earlier projects, including unit appliqué and small dimensional flowers. The new techniques introduced for the first time in this project are reverse appliqué (used for the iris petals), and the use of a bias maker to construct the woven basket. As in previous projects I always like to suggest alternative ideas for stitching the designs. For this project a quick way to construct the basket is to use purchased fusible bias binding instead of making your own with the bias maker; the fusible binding is available in a wide range of colours, but you would need to find a co-ordinating fabric for the base. The weaving is easily fused in position before stitching.*

*Use shaded batik fabrics for the flowers to give a 'painterly' look to the flowers and buds. I used one fabric for the basket, and by fussy-cutting it I was able to achieve a contrast between the weaving strips and the ribs, to show off the weaving pattern, but you could use two different fabrics instead. Batik is also a good choice of fabric for using with a bias maker to get a crisp finish on the strips.*

*Spring Basket is a 'masterclass' for hand appliqué. This final needle-turned design takes me back to my appliqué roots, when I first started designing and stitching in the Baltimore style but giving the genre an English twist!*

**Finished size:** *The design measures approx 12 x 11in*

## What you will need:

- 16in square background fabric
- for the appliqué:
  - 8 x 10in of two co-ordinating fabrics, for the basket and ribs and the weaving strips (or, if you wish, you can use the same fabric for both ribs and weaving strips)
  - small piece for the basket lining
  - small pieces of fabric in the following colours:
    - 3-4 toning greens for the leaves and stems
    - colours of your choice for the tulips
    - a shaded green for the tulip buds
    - tones of purple/mauve for the irises plus a little yellow
    - shaded pink for the clematis Montana plus a little pale yellow
    - light blues/mauves for the forget-me-nots
- silk thread or alternative fine thread to match the appliqué fabrics
- freezer paper for templates
- stranded embroidery thread in pale yellow and green
- ¼in bias maker
- spray starch

## Preparation

**1** Mark the centre lines on background with small tacking stitches (see p12); follow the instructions on p12 to make an overlay and attach it in position.

**2**  Prepare the numbered freezer paper templates – there are 87 for this design, so only cut them out as needed! Group and store them in little plastic bags. As you get to each stage of the design, use the freezer paper templates to prepare and cut the relevant fabric shapes ready for appliqué.

## Appliqué

### Basket

**3**  Appliqué the base (#1), leaving the top edge raw; be careful to keep the lower edge of the base straight on the background fabric.

**4**  Trace the template for the basket lining (#2) onto freezer paper; cut it out, and iron it onto the right side of the basket lining fabric. Cut out the shape without adding any seam allowance. Use the overlay to position the basket lining on the background, lining it up with the dotted line; the lining sits just inside the outer edge of the basket. Secure the lining in place with running stitches around the edge.

**5**  Spray-starch the fabric for the basket ribs and weaving strips – this makes it easier to use with the bias maker. Cut bias strips a scant ⅝in wide – some from each fabric if you are using two fabrics; cut just a few to start with, then cut more as needed. Cut the ends of the bias strips diagonally, as this makes it easier to start feeding the strips through the bias maker. Take one bias strip and feed it through bias maker at the wide end until about ¼in emerges from the narrow end; the side edges will now be folded in (**a**). It sometimes helps to use a pin to push the strip through at the start (**b**). Keep moving the

a

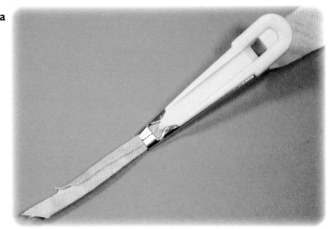

b

bias maker along to feed through more of the strip, and press firmly with the iron, close to the bias maker, where the strip emerges. Try not to stretch the strip. Pressing on a firm ironing surface helps to get a crisp finish

**6**  You may find it helpful to place the work on a soft surface such as cork, foam or padded board while you assemble the basket. Use the outline of the basket lining to position the ribs; pin each rib at the top and the base.

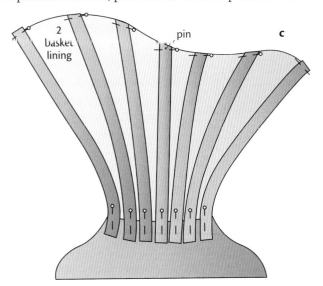

2 Basket lining — pin — c

**TIP: You can use a small piece of fusible web at the top of each rib to hold in place during the weaving.**

The ribs should line up with the top of the lining, but leave an extra ½in at the base – this will be trimmed back later. Place the centre rib and the outer ribs first, checking with the overlay that the outer ones are in the correct position, then place two more ribs between the central one and the outer rib on each side (**c**); pin all the ribs in position. Weave the basket; use the design as guide for placing the horizontal weaving strips. Extend the weavers for an extra inch beyond the sides of basket; the surplus will be trimmed back later. Tack the outer ribs in position, and also tack all the ribs firmly across the base end. Stitch the inner edge of the outside ribs, stopping at the base; trim the excess off the weavers, underneath the outside ribs (**d**).

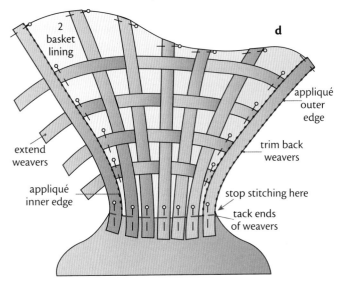

2 basket lining — d — appliqué outer edge — extend weavers — trim back weavers — appliqué inner edge — stop stitching here — tack ends of weavers

**7**  Stitch down the outer edges of the outside ribs, starting ¼in from the top on the left-hand side only, and stopping both lines of stitching just above the basket base; this will enable you to tuck the final strip (which covers the lower ends of the ribs) neatly under at the outside edges of the basket. Make any final adjustments to the ribs and weavers to space them evenly – overlap the ribs neatly at the base if necessary to fit. Tack or lightly glue all the bias strips in place

**8**  Take a prepared bias strip and place it on the left hand side of the top edge, covering the raw edge of the basket lining. Leave an extra ¼in at the start, and extend ¼in under the position of leaf 17 – use the overlay to check the position of the leaf. The remaining top edge of the basket will be covered by the other leaves and the flowers. Stitch the strip in place, turning the raw end at the start under the outside rib (**e**).

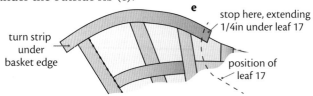

e — stop here, extending 1/4in under leaf 17 — turn strip under basket edge — position of leaf 17

**9** Place a prepared bias strip over the ends of the ribs, as shown on the design, extending ¼in at each end; appliqué the top edge of the strip only (**f**). Trim the ends of the ribs so that the strip will cover the raw edges. Tuck the ends of the strip under the end ribs to neaten, them, and finish stitching the strip in position.

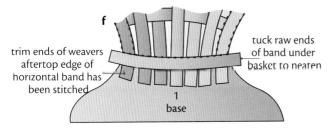

trim ends of weavers after top edge of horizontal band has been stitched

tuck raw ends of band under basket to neaten

**f**

1 base

**10** You will need to catch down some of the weaving; later quilting will shrink the background a little, and this will cause the weaving to become loose if it's not stitched to the background. A few strategic stitches will help to keep everything in place while still retaining the 3D texture of the weaving.

**11** Appliqué the basket handle (#3a) and separate small section (#3b).

### Leaves and stems

**12** Appliqué leaf section #4 as one piece – the stem (#6) is stitched on top. To keep things easy, use the separate template. Then appliqué leaf #5.

**13** Cut ¾in-wide bias strips for the stems (#6-11) and appliqué them using the fine stem method (see p27). Fold each bias strip in half, wrong sides together, and use the overlay to position it on the background with the folded edge on the outer curve of the stem. Allow ⅛in extra at each end to be covered later by adjacent shapes.

**14** Appliqué the remaining leaves (#12-20) in number order. Pre-assemble leaf #15/16 using unit appliqué as shown in the sequence of diagrams (**g**), then stitch it to the background; this gives the leaf a smooth outer edge.

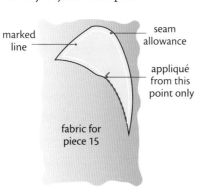

marked line

seam allowance

appliqué from this point only

fabric for piece 15

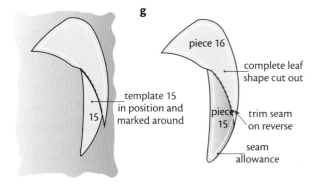

**g**

template 15 in position and marked around

15

piece 16

complete leaf shape cut out

piece 15

trim seam on reverse

seam allowance

### Irises

**15** Appliqué shapes #21 and 22, using a green fabric.

**16** I used reverse appliqué to achieve the distinctive yellow markings on the iris petals (#50, 51, 55, 56, 59-61); some of the yellow details are very small shapes, which would have been almost impossible to needleturn using the usual method. For reverse appliqué, two layers of fabric are used and the top layer is cut away in areas to reveal the fabric underneath. The cut edges of the top layer fabric are needle-turned in the usual way.

> **TIP:** An alternative method for creating the yellow marks on the petals is to fuse the yellow patches in place; you can then straight stitch these details, or just leave the edges raw as the patches are very small. Add the markings to the petals before cutting out the petals as shown.

**17** To make the petals follow the technique shown in the sequence of diagrams (**h**), which show petal #51. Iron the petal template onto the right side of the purple fabric and mark round the shape in the usual way (**h1**). Cut out the shape, adding a seam allowance, and remove the template (**h2**). Pin the petal to a piece of yellow fabric and cut centrally between the marked lines (as show by the dotted line), cutting through the purple fabric only (**h3**). If you pin each side of the cut before stitching, this will help the edges to stay in position; needle-turn around the cut (**h4**) to reveal the yellow fabric underneath – clip the seam allowance slightly if you want to achieve a slight curve on the marking. Don't worry if the shape gets a little distorted; the markings can vary – mine did. On the reverse of the petal, trim the yellow fabric away fairly close to the stitching for a flat finish (**h5**).

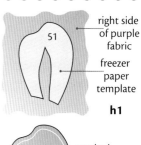

51

right side of purple fabric

freezer paper template

**h1**

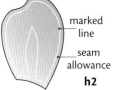

marked line

seam allowance

**h2**

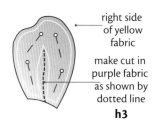

right side of yellow fabric

make cut in purple fabric as shown by dotted line

**h3**

**h4**

appliqué each edge of cut

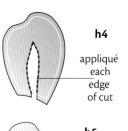

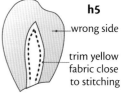

**h5**

wrong side

trim yellow fabric close to stitching

Press the petal, then iron the freezer paper template back in place so that you can use the overlay to position the petal accurately on the background.

**18** Appliqué the irises at the top left and the top right, working through the shapes in number order. Use lighter tones for #52, 53, 57 and 58 to give definition to each flower (**i**).

i

**19** For the centre iris, use the separate templates given for petals #59-61; make and appliqué them as in step 17. Prepare shapes 62, 63 and 64 using a lighter tone of fabric, then appliqué them in position. For the flower centre, cut a 1in circle of fabric and work a running stitch close to the edge; pull it up tightly and flatten it to make a circle, then appliqué it in the centre of the iris.

### Tulips

There are four different styles of tulips in the basket. Fussy-cut the fabrics to create shading on the petals and to give definition to each flower.

**20** Appliqué the left-hand tulip in the usual way, using templates #24–27. Note that the central petal (27) is slightly lower at the base than the side petals; this means that it can neatly cover the seam allowance of the side petals. Appliqué the top tulip in the same way using templates #31-34.

**21** You will find it best to use unit appliqué for the remaining tulips, as they all have seams running to the outer edge of the flower. Unit appliqué enables you to turn the seam allowances under smoothly at the outer edges. You might find it helpful to make a little plastic overlay of each tulip (see p13) to check that the pieces are lined up correctly while you're making the units; the plastic also helps you to choose specific fabric shading for the individual petals.

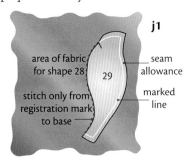

j1

area of fabric for shape 28
seam allowance
29
stitch only from registration mark to base
marked line

**22** The sequence of diagrams (**j**) shows pre-assembling one of the tulips using templates #28-30. Use the

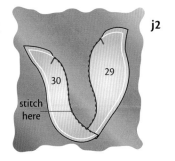

j2

29
30
stitch here

registration marks to line up the shapes, and so that you can see where to start stitching shapes 29 and 30 onto the fabric you've chosen for piece 28 (**j1-4**). Trim the seams on the back to detach the unit from the fabric (**j5**). Appliqué the assembled tulip to the background, sweeping under the seam allowances at the base in a graceful curve.

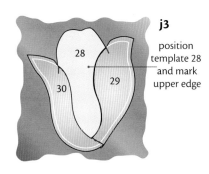

j3

28
29
30
position template 28 and mark upper edge

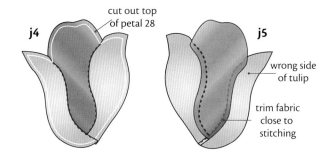

j4
cut out top of petal 28

j5
wrong side of tulip
trim fabric close to stitching

**23** Appliqué shape #39 to the background. Pre-assemble shapes 40 and 41 as shown in the sequence of diagrams (**k**), then appliqué the assembled unit in position over shape 39 on the background (**l**).

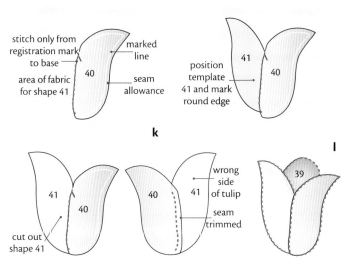

stitch only from registration mark to base
marked line
area of fabric for shape 41
40
seam allowance

position template 41 and mark round edge
41
40

k

41
40
cut out shape 41

40
41
wrong side of tulip
seam trimmed

l
39

**24** Appliqué shape #35 to the background. Use unit appliqué to pre-assemble petals #36-38, then cut out the shape and appliqué it; do the same for the final tulip, using templates #42-45.

### Tulip buds

**25** I used a green fabric with a coloured shading for the tulip buds. Plain green just didn't look right, so I checked a photo of tulip buds just about to open and found I needed to show the colour coming through. A hint of colour in the buds balanced the design much better. Appliqué buds #46-48 in the usual way.

## Clematis

**26** Use the master template (A) for all the clematis flower petals. I lined the flowers to give more colour density and to prevent any background showing through. Lining also produced a slightly raised effect on the appliqué; however it's your choice whether you think it's necessary. If you do decide to line the flowers, take a piece of white cotton fabric and back it with fusible web. Use the pattern window of the master pattern and draw inside the window to mark twenty petal shapes on the paper side of the web-backed lining fabric. Cut out the linings. (For more about lined appliqué see p98-99.)

**27** Cut out a clematis petal, using the master template and adding the usual seam allowance. Mark round the shape and leave the template in position. Peel the paper backing off a lining shape. If you hold the petal up to the light you will be able to see the template through it, which will enable you to line up the lining on the reverse. Fuse the lining in place. Make all the petals in the same way. Position the clematis petals on the background, and appliqué them in place.

**28** To make the fringed centre for each flower, cut a strip of yellow fabric ¼ x 2½in on the straight grain of the fabric. Work a line of running stitch along one long edge, starting ¼in from each end (**m**) and overlapping the ends

1/4in                  **m**     1/4in

by ¼in to form a ring (**n**). Pull up the gathers tightly and fasten off the thread; fray the outer edge of the strip. Stitch this shape to the centre of the flower, using a few French

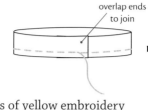

overlap ends to join

**n**

knots worked with two strands of yellow embroidery thread. Make all five clematis flowers in the same way.

**29** Appliqué the clematis buds #65-67. Embroider the clematis stems, using stem stitch and two strands of green embroidery thread.

### Forget-me-nots

**30** Cut ten 1in circles in a mixture of pale blue and mauve fabrics. Follow the instructions on p36 to make these into Suffolk Puff flowers, dividing each circle into three petals, and embroider a French knot in the centre of each flower using two strands of embroidery thread. Refer to the photo and the full-size design for the placement of the flowers, and stitch them in position.

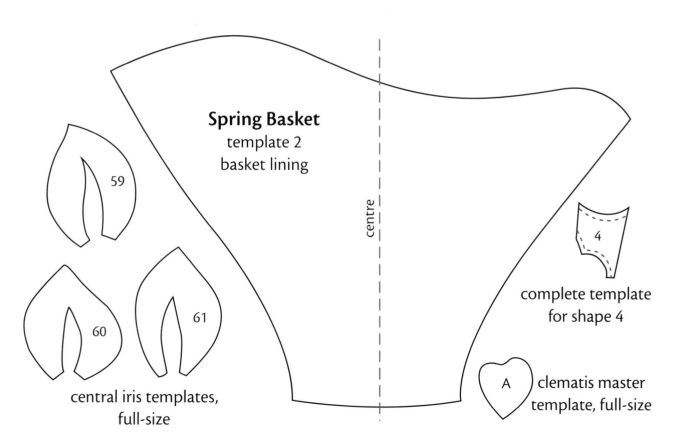

59

60     61

central iris templates, full-size

**Spring Basket**
template 2
basket lining

centre

4

complete template for shape 4

A   clematis master template, full-size

*The grand finale*     **117**

position of
forget-me-nots

**Spring basket**
full-size design

centre

centre

*The grand finale*

# *Finishing touches*

Having put so much time and effort into stitching your appliqué design, it deserves the extra care to make it into a beautiful finished project. In this section I'll take you through the construction stages, and also offer general techniques and ideas for borders, quilting and binding. (Specific instructions for borders and quilting are given for each project.)

## Pressing

Press the work from the back on a well-padded surface. The background areas around the appliqué may be pressed more heavily, but press the appliqué only lightly: heavy pressing will flatten the texture of hand appliqué, and cause the seam allowances to leave an impression on the right side.

## Cutting to size

◇ A 15in-square ruler is very useful for squaring up the work accurately after the appliqué is complete. Trim the work accurately using a rotary cutter on a cutting mat.

◇ If the work has lots of dimensional details it can be difficult to lay the ruler flat on the surface. To avoid this problem, here's a great tip from Nancy Kerns. Make a card 'window' template the required finished size plus seam allowance. Mark a line 1in inside each edge, and cut out the inner square to leave a central hole; mark the centre of the square on each side of the card. You now have a frame that you can place centrally over the block (**a**). Draw round the outer edge of the card template; remove the card template, and trim the work on the marked line.

**a**

## Settings and Borders

◇ How you choose to set and border your appliqué is an important design decision which can greatly enhance the finished work. First, consider whether the design is to be set straight or 'on point' – turning the square at 45°. The hand appliquéd version of *Robin Wreath* was set straight, but I added a pieced red and green border to create a secondary pattern. The fused version of the same design was placed on point, and this has given me the opportunity for a different style of framing. (Whether to place the design on the straight or on point is of course a decision you need to make before stitching the project!)

◇ Although most appliqué panels and blocks benefit from a border, there are others that would look too constrained by a border. The *Lily Pond* quilt (p45) is one good example – the simple binding in the same fabric as the background neatens the edge of the quilt but doesn't create a definite cut-off point to the scene. Another way to 'free' the design is to extend some elements of the design into the border. *Sunflowers and Butterflies* quilt (p62) uses this device – the dimensional fence in the foreground continues into the border.

◇ It's always worth 'auditioning' various fabrics for borders, and you may find that a double border works better than a single one. I often make a narrow inner border using one of the appliqué fabrics, and then a wider outer border which reflects the general colour scheme but is not too dominant (for instance the *Cyclamen Pot* design on p70). To audition fabrics for borders, fold the fabrics so that the appropriate amount of each one shows against the quilt (below). This is often the best stage to decide on whether to use one or more borders, and to see the best width of border to give balance to the quilt. If you have a design wall it's useful to pin the fabrics up and stand back to consider the colour combinations. The appliqué is the focus of the quilt, so you want the borders to frame the design and draw the eye in to the appliqué.

### Inserting narrow borders

A ¼in narrow inner border really sets off the appliqué – a bit like a double mount for a photograph or painting. The disadvantage is that because it **is** so narrow, any unevenness in the width is very visible. The method I use overcomes that problem.

**1** Cut two strips of border fabric 1in wide and the length of the quilt sides plus seam allowances; press the strip accurately in half along its length, right sides out.

**2** Open out one strip and pin it to a side edge of your quilt or block, right sides together and matching raw edges (**a**). Machine along the fold line; this will give you a ½in seam (**b**). Fold the strip in half over the machine stitching and press (**c**). Use the same method to attach the second strip to the other side of the quilt. Cut two 1in strips the required length for the top and bottom edges and attach them in the same way (**d**).

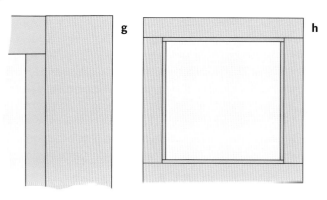

### Shaped borders

◇ Shaped borders can echo the theme or style of the appliqué design. The informal wavy border of *Midnight Dance* (p54) reflects the quirky nature of the design and adds further movement, whereas the more formal style of *Just a Perfect Day* (**a**) is enhanced by a shaped and trapunto-quilted border to suggest a heavily -carved old picture frame. The shaped border on *Woodland Foxgloves* (**b**) was fussy-cut to echo the foxglove colours in the border.

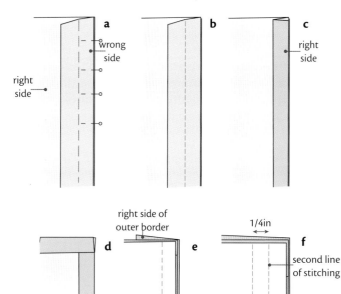

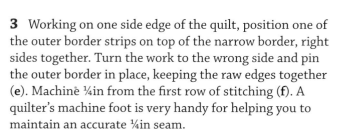

**3** Working on one side edge of the quilt, position one of the outer border strips on top of the narrow border, right sides together. Turn the work to the wrong side and pin the outer border in place, keeping the raw edges together (**e**). Machine ¼in from the first row of stitching (**f**). A quilter's machine foot is very handy for helping you to maintain an accurate ¼in seam.

**4** On the right side, press the seam towards the border. You now have an accurate inner border sandwiched between the block and outer border (**g**). Add the outer border to the opposite side in the same way, and then add the top and bottom borders (**h**).

◇ To make a shaped border, cut a freezer paper template for each side. Appliqué the inner edges of the side borders first to the background, and then appliqué the inner edges of the top and bottom borders. The borders on *Just a Perfect Day* were mitred at the corners, but usually you can take the top and bottom borders straight across. If you are planning to add shaped borders, ensure that you cut the background fabric large enough to extend at least 1in under the borders at the narrowest part of the shaped border. (See also the border instructions for *Midnight Dance*.)

### Multiple borders

◇ Two or three (or more) borders can often enlarge a single block to make it into a more impressive quilt – my quilt *Summertime* (**a**) is an example. The central block is framed by a narrow border, to separate it from the appliquéd borders which have the same background fabric. An appliquéd dog-tooth border completes the quilt – note that I used a slightly deeper tone of the background fabric for this border.

◇ Two or three borders in toning prints usually work better than one very wide one; the borders on *Spring Glade* are a good example (**b**). *Sunflowers and Butterflies* (p62) has a contrasting inner border to bring forward the centre design against the outer green border. Add a ¾-1in border first, followed by a 2-3in-wide one – the exact widths will depend on the size of your quilt.

a

b

### Marking quilting designs

Depending on the way that you've chosen to quilt your project, you may want to trace on a quilting design once you've added the border(s). You can also use a hera to mark quilting lines at this stage, with the work laid on a cutting mat, which is much easier than trying to mark the design after you've layered the quilt. (You will find ideas for background quilting on p123.)

## Layering and quilting

A quilt has three layers – the top, wadding/batting and backing. There are many brands and types of wadding but for an appliquéd quilt, a flat, low-loft wadding works best. Hobbs Heirloom® cotton/polyester batting is one example. Quilters Dream® cotton (Request loft) also works well, and Thermore®, a polyester wadding, is a very thin wadding. Some waddings need to be washed before you use them due to shrinkage, so check the packaging information.

### Making the quilt 'sandwich'

**1** Cut the wadding 1in bigger all round than the quilt top, and cut the backing fabric the same size as the wadding. If you are hand quilting, use a soft cotton fabric for the backing; batiks, being tightly woven, are more difficult to hand quilt.

**2** Make the quilt sandwich. Lay the backing fabric, right side down, on a flat work surface; on large pieces, tape the backing to the surface to keep it held flat. Position the

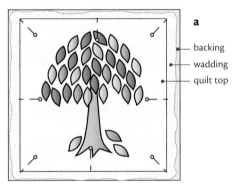

a

backing
wadding
quilt top

wadding on top, and finally lay on the quilt top, right side up. Smooth out the layers and pin the quilt sandwich in the centre, and at the centre of the outer edges (**a**).

**3** If you intend to hand quilt the top, you will need to tack the layers together in a grid formation. If you intend to machine quilt, then you could use safety pins to hold the layers together. However, as I'm usually quilting small pieces rather

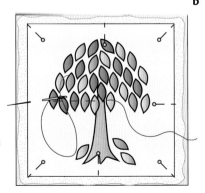

b

than bed quilts, I still usually tack the layers and clip the stitches if they are in the way when machining. Start the tacking at the centre, leaving a long tail of thread; you

can then re-thread the tail to tack in the opposite direction later (**b**). Tack the centre lines to start with, and then complete the grid working outwards from the centre lines as shown (**c**).

c

## Quilting tips

◇ There is a wonderful array of quilting threads available today – I particularly like the shaded and variegated ones as the quilting blends with the background fabric, emphasising the texture and adding subtle colour effects. These threads can be used for both machine and hand quilting. I also use regular 40 cotton machine thread for hand quilting rather than the 'proper' hand quilting thread, as I find the latter rather thick. For fairly dense free motion quilting, as well as small (½ or ¼in) quilted grids, YLI #100 silk threads are excellent, as you can achieve the texture without the stitching being too dominant (see the fused version of *Robin Wreath* on p87). Experiment with different threads to see which you prefer for particular effects.

◇ When you are machine quilting, use a walking foot on your sewing machine if your machine doesn't have a built-in even-feed facility. Also use a machine quilting needle: a size 75 suits medium-thickness threads.

◇ Outline-quilt the appliqué design by hand or machine, stitching a scant ⅛in from the appliqué. This helps to bring the appliqué forward and gives it more dimension. You may need to quilt in vein lines on leaves, division lines between petals, and possibly additional designs on large pieces such as vases to give more definition to the appliqué. The extra quilting on large pieces also helps to keep them flat – see the vase on *Midnight Dance* (p54), and the leaves on *Lily Pond* (p45).

◇ There are various ways to quilt the background of your design, but remember that appliqué – especially hand appliqué – generally sits better if the background is fairly well quilted. Also, try to keep an even density of quilting over the whole quilt, including the borders on larger quilts, otherwise the quilt edges tend to flute and the quilt doesn't hang very well.

## Background quilting ideas

◇ A pattern of square diamonds or diagonal lines, worked by hand or machine, is classic. Lines of this kind can be marked with the aid of the hera (**a**) so that there's no problem removing pencil marks.

a
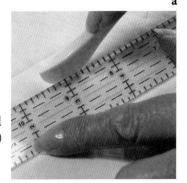

◇ Hand echo-quilting also works well with appliqué. Quilt rows of stitching, echoing the appliqué design – if these rows are worked close together they can create an interesting stipple effect (see *Spring Glade* on p122).

◇ It can look very attractive to incorporate some of the shapes that were used for the appliqué into the background quilting (**b** and **c**); pin the templates onto the background and either stitch round the shapes, or draw round the shapes with removable marker and then remove the templates and stitch.

b
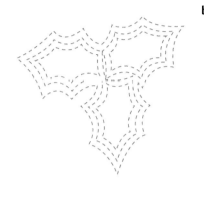

c

◇ Try stitching French knots in a random pattern to give a stippled effect. Use either a regular sewing thread or two strands of stranded embroidery floss for a bolder effect (**d**).

d

◇ Use the appliqué templates to make a quilting design; on *Robin Wreath* (p80) I used the ivy templates to quilt the green border.

◇ Flowing irregular quilted lines, either stitched as free-motion quilting or worked with a walking foot, can suggest landscape or water as well as a general background texture (see *Lily Pond* on p45).

## Continuous binding

### Preparation

Quilting tends to shrink the work slightly, so once the quilting is complete, trim the quilt to an accurate rectangle. Lay the quilt flat on a table and work running stitch around the edge to keep the layers together – you can also ease in any fullness at this stage if the quilt does not lie quite flat.

### Adding a double binding

One of the challenges faced by quilters when binding a quilt is to get accurate mitred corners. This method, using a continuous binding strip, works well and makes very good, easy mitres.

**1** The width of the finished binding needs to be in proportion to the size of the quilt. For most wall quilts a ⅜in-wide finished binding is about right – on a very small one this could be reduced to ¼in. Cut the binding strips on the crosswise grain of the fabric as this has a little 'give' for a smooth finished binding (**a**) – you only need cut the strips on the bias if the edge is curved and shaped.

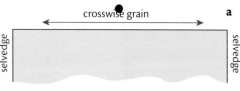

**2** The width of the binding strip needs to be six times the finished width plus a little extra to allow for the thickness of the quilt. The aim is for the binding to fit snugly over the raw edges. So, for instance, for a ⅜in finished binding cut the strip 2⅜in wide.

**3** To determine the required length, measure round the quilt, then add on about 12in for the corner turns and the final join. You will probably have to make at least one join to create a long enough strip.

**4** Join the strips on the bias to give a flatter finish. Place two strips right sides together as shown (**b**), and use a short machine stitch to stitch a seam (**c**); you may like to pencil in a line for guidance. Press the seam open and trim (**d**).

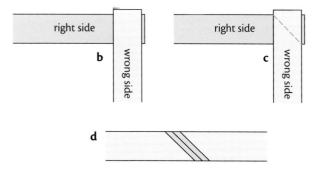

**5** Fold the binding strip in half, wrong sides facing, and lightly press. Before you begin pinning the binding to the quilt it's a good idea to place the binding round the edge of quilt to check where the joins in the strip will come – try to avoid having a join at a corner.

**6** Begin in the centre of one side of the quilt. Lay the strip on the quilt, raw edges together; mark with a pin where the strip starts. (Leave the pin in place – you will need this position later when you make the final join in the binding.) Pin the strip along the edge of the quilt, right sides together, pinning at right angles (**e**). When you come to the end of the first side, fold back the binding level with the edge of the quilt and crease it firmly.

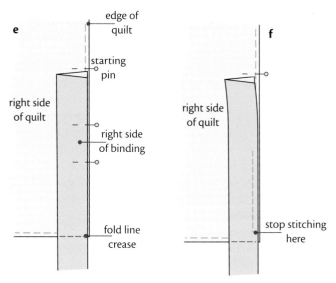

**7** Use a walking foot to stitch on the binding; leave at least 6in of the binding strip free before starting the machine stitching – you need quite a long tail for making the final join. Taking a scant ⅜in seam, machine the strip in place, stopping a scant ⅜in from the fold (**f**). (I measure and mark the spot with a small dot to show me where to stop.) Secure with a few reverse stitches.

> TIP: It's a good idea to stitch just a few inches of the binding in place and then take the work out of the machine, to check that the binding strip will fold over to the back to meet the stitching line, and that the binding fits snugly over the edge. If necessary, change the needle position or slightly change the fabric position so that you can achieve the correct seam allowance. The thickness of the binding fabric and the quilt sandwich can make a slight difference to the seam allowance required for a good fit.

**8** To make the mitre, fold up the strip at 45° so that the folded crease line lies along the edge of the quilt (**g**). Now fold the strip down so that it lies along the adjacent edge (**h**). You will see that a diagonal fold has been formed under the strip, which will create a mitre at the corner. Pin the binding strip in place down the adjacent side, making a crease as before at the next corner. Re-start machining from the edge of the work and stop as before to create a mitre at the next corner.

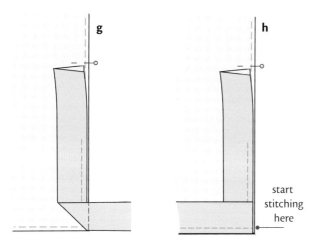

**9** Continue in the same way until you have turned all four corners. Machine part-way along the final side, stopping 4in from the starting pin. You now need to join the strip before going any further, and this can sometimes be a bit tricky; however, the method I describe here works really well every time, giving a perfect fit! Overlap the tail end of the binding with the start of the binding. On the tail end measure the width of the binding strip (in this case 2⅜in) from the pin which you placed at the start. Mark this measurement on the binding strip (**i**). Cut off the **tail end only** at the marked point (**j**) – do not cut the start. Open up the binding at the start, then fold down the corner diagonally and make a crease on the fold (**k**); this will be the seam line for the join.

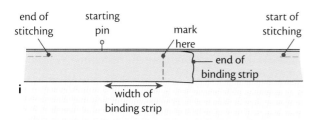

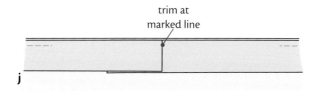

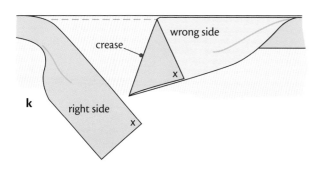

Open up the tail end of the binding and place the two ends of the binding together at right angles, right sides facing as shown (**l**).

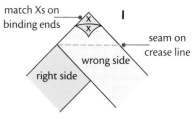

Pin and stitch the seam on the creased line. Refold the binding and check that it fits the remaining quilt edge; if necessary adjust the seam, but if you have measured accurately there should be no problems. Trim the seam to ⅛in and press it open; re-fold the binding, pin it to the quilt edge, and machine it in position.

**10** Finally, fold the binding to the back, and hem the folded edge to the machine stitching. Arrange the folds in a mitre at each corner on the back (**m**). You have now successfully completed your quilt. Add a hanging sleeve to display a wall quilt and a label to record the date and who made the quilt.

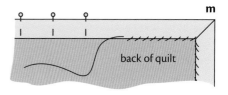

## Piping

A piped seam is an attractive and practical seam finish for a cushion or bag. I used it to finish the edge of the *Daisy Meadow* cushion (**a**).

**1** You can buy piping cord in various thicknesses – choose the size appropriate for your project. It's advisable to wash cotton piping before use, as it does shrink. Cut bias strips of fabric 1¼in wide – you may need wider strips for thicker cords, as the bias strip needs to cover the cord and still leave a seam allowance on each side. Join the bias strips (see p124) to give you sufficient length to fit around cushion plus at least 3in for the final join.

**2** Place the cord centrally on the wrong side of the bias strip and fold the strip over. Pin the bias strip in position a few inches at a time, and either machine stitch or use a small running stitch close to the cord. If you're stitching by machine, use the zipper foot attachment and try to

keep the cord snugly covered with the bias strip. If you

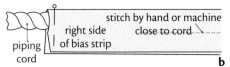

need to make a continuous piping, for example round a cushion, start stitching about 4in along (**b**) and stop about 6in from the end. Trim the seam allowance to ¼in.

**3**  This is the traditional way to make a continuous piped edge where the join doesn't show, but it can be a little tricky. (Try the alternative method given in step 5 if you are not too confident about piping.) Pin the piping to the right side of the cushion front, starting in the centre of one side; the cut edges of the bias should be level with the outside edge of the cushion. Ease the piping round the corner, clipping the

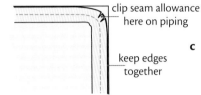

seam allowance a little on the piping covering to keep the piping and the cushion flat at the corners (**c**).

**4**  To join the piping cord, check the length to fit around the cushion and add ½in, and trim the cord to that length. Unravel both ends of the cord for ½in and trim away some of the loose strands. Twist the remaining strands tightly together, maintaining the correct length; bind the ends together with a few stitches (**d**). Check the length of the bias

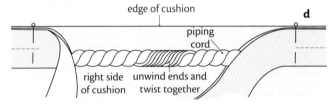

strips and make a final join on the straight grain (see p124 – step 4 of **Adding a double binding**). Re-fold the bias strip over the piping cord and complete the stitching. Pin the piping to the right side of the cushion front, keeping all the raw edges together. Tack close to the original machine stitching to position piping securely all round the edges of the cushion.

**5**  For the alternative method, prepare a length of piping (as in step 1) long enough to go round cushion plus an extra 4in. For this method you don't need to leave the ends of the binding strip unstitched. Pin the covered piping in position all round cushion as in step 4 above, starting half-way along one side; place the first 2in of piping over the edge (**e**). Keep all the outer raw edges level as you pin, and clip corners as in step 4. To finish at the end, simply overlap

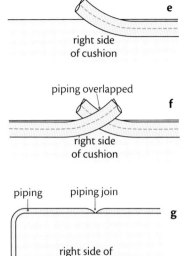

the piping overlapping as shown (**f**). Tack the piping in place on the cushion stitching as in step 4 above. The diagram (**g**) shows the finished appearance of the join; although it's not invisible, it still looks very neat and is easier to make.

**6**  Once the piping is in place, put the cushion front and cushion back right sides together, sandwiching the piping between. Pin the edges together with the raw edges matching. If the cushion has a zip fastening in the back undo the zip a little. Use the machine zipper foot and stitch a ¼ seam around the cushion, keeping the stitching close to the piping. You may find that a generous ¼in seam works best to ensure that the stitching is close to the piping. Open the zip fully and turn the cushion cover through to the right side.

# Circle templates

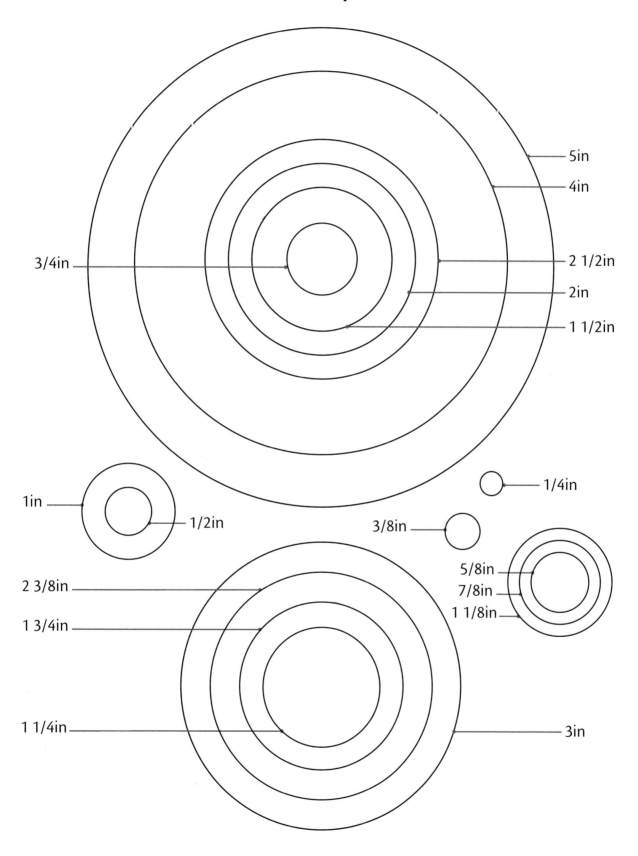

# The last word

## Resources

YLI ™ silk threads,
Clover™ appliqué pins,
Clover ™ white marking pens and
Sewline™ fabric pencils
are available from many quilt shops including:

Sew & So's
14, Upper Olland Street,
Bungay, Suffolk NR35 1BG

www.sewsos.co.uk

Overlay material is available from Sew and So's

Straws #11 (Milliners') needles are available from
Sew & So's and Little L Fabrics (www.littlelfab.co.uk)

Mylar ™ circles are available from
Brandy's www.brandysquiltpatterns.com,
Creative Grids www.creativegrids.com, and Sew and So's

## Acknowledgements

The Christmas roses and the rose on the cream bag (p39)
were made by Muriel Fitch. All the other projects and
samples in this book have been designed, appliquéd and
quilted by Shirley.

My grateful thanks to my husband, Colin, who with great
patience took many of the photographs for this book.

I would also like to thank Chris and Gail Lawther of
Teamwork Craftbooks for all their generous help and
support in producing the book.

## About the author

Shirley trained in Textiles and Design and taught in
High Schools for 23 years. For the past 15 years she
has developed her interest in hand appliqué, inspired
by the Baltimore Album Quilts and developing her
own designs to give Baltimore an English Twist. She
regularly contributes designs to quilting magazines
and publishes the **Country Pleasures** pattern range.
Shirley gives talks and teaches workshops and
residential courses throughout the UK, as well as
further a field in the US, France, Ireland and Spain.
Her first book, **The Appliqué Garden,** was published by
Teamwork Craftbooks in 2006 and focused on hand
appliqué; it is now out of print. In this, her second
book, she has extended the scope to include other
appliqué methods.

*Just a Perfect Day*, *Summertime*, *Woodland Foxgloves* and
*Spring Glade,* which are shown in the *Finishing Touches*
section, are four examples from the **Country Pleasures**
pattern range.

Patterns may be ordered direct from her at
www.shirleybloomfield.co.uk,

or e-mail for more information:
shirley@shirleybloomfield.co.uk

*The last word*